ROLE OF SEX IN TOURISM DEVELOPMENT

ROLE OF SEX IN TOURISM DEVELOPMENT

Vinod Goel

2008

CYBER TECH PUBLICATIONS
4264/3, Ansari Road, Daryaganj, New Delhi-110002 (India)
Ph.: 011-23244078. Fax: 011-23280028
E-Mail: cyberpublicationsdelhi@yahoo.com

ROLE OF SEX IN TOURISM DEVELOPMENT

Vinod Goel

First Edition 2008

Published by :

G.S. Rawat for **Cyber Tech Publications**
4264/3, Ansari Road, Daryaganj, New Delhi-110002 (India)
Ph.: 011-23244078. Fax: 011-23280028
E-Mail: cyberpublicationsdelhi@yahoo.com

Printed at : **Amit Enterprises**, Maujpur, Delhi, (9810878184)

Preface

The sex services industry has been expressed by local patriotic and church women's groups in the host countries. Some westerners have viewed the phenomenon with interest because it seems even more exotic than other popular images of Asia and Asian cultures. Moreover, the group behaviour of Japanese male sex tourists strikes many Americans and Europeans as odd, even comical. But the real significance of sex tourism is political and economic as well as cultural: sex tourism reflects the unequal political and economic relationship between developing and industrialized nations and between the sexes on a worldwide scale.

The continued economic gap between many nations in East and Southeast Asia and the wealthy nations in the West and Japan a gap resulting from decades of war and colonial rule, makes the most valued commodity in South Korea, Taiwan, Hong Kong, and the Philippines continue to be low-wage skilled, semi-skilled, and unskilled labour in foreign controlled industries.

—Author

Contents

1

PROSTITUTION AND SEX IN TOURISM

INTRODUCTDION

Travelling has become a part of everyday life in many societies of todays world. Crossing a border has lost its magic for many people, thus making foreign and domestic travel in their minds more and more alike. However, this does not change a basic reality, namely that travel to a foreign country is not a neutral action.

International visitors should therefore enter a foreign country with sensitivity to cultural, ethnic, social, economic or religious differences between their country of origin and should respect the values that these differences entail in the host country. This is especially evident in sexual customs. What is acceptable behaviour in one country (e.g. public displays of affection or nudity) may be quite unacceptable and even illegal in another. Sexual mores require particular sensitivity from tourists.

Historically, travel and prostitution have often been associated. The earliest tourism destinations were religious shrines or trade centres and in the ruins of ancient cities such as Ephesus, Babylon and Pompeii prostitute quarters are still clearly visible and surprisingly large. Inveterate travellers in history, particularly seamen and soldiers, have helped to create a place for prostitution in the cities they visited. Today the number of tourists is increasing dramatically. Most of these new travellers are not deliberately seeking sex when they travel but even so the number who make use of commercial sex is considerable, especially in those destinations where sexual services are readily available.

There are many psychological as well as social and cultural reasons advanced to explain why this takes place:

- When the tourist is away from home there is an anonymity which releases him or her from the usual social restraints which determine behaviour in the home country. A man who would never contemplate visiting a brothel in his home town will often do so in a foreign country where there is little likelihood of detection. Many countries have noted this phenomena. A Japanese proverb claims that the traveller knows no shame". A common saying in parts of Europe is, "the further I go from home the less moral I become".

- In .exotic" tourist destinations visitors usually cannot understand the language or the cultural nuances in the society. This leads them to make assumptions which are probably untrue but which enable them to rationalise their changed behaviour. It is common for those tourists who sexually exploit children to explain their behaviour by saying that sex with children "is more acceptable in this culture, and the people here do not have the same sexual hang-ups we have in our country". Equally common among exploiters is the rationalisation that this is a way of helping poor children to get some money.

- Tourism does not only change behaviour, it can also reinforce prejudice. Visitors who hold strong views, whether explicit or obscure, about the inferiority of people other than their own usually have their racist attitudes reinforced in foreign countries. They see what they want to see. Such people have no scruples about exploiting other persons because they consider them to be inferior.

- The experience of economic superiority in a poorer country tempts some visitors to sexually exploit and abuse local people. Modern tourists from industrialised nations may hold quite menial positions in their own country but the disparity in salaries can mean they are comparatively wealthy when they travel to a poor country. These nouveau riche will sometimes spend their money in sexual activities which they have associated with the rich and the famous.

- Tourists are sometimes fleeing from an unhappy sexual relationship at home and are open to new sexual experiences. Aspects of this have been noted among men from Western industrialised societies. With traditional privileges of patriarchal society slowly being closed off in many Western countries some men feel inadequate to cope with the change. Marriages and other relationships break down, employment opportunities are no longer so readily available and strong. women are seen to be a threat to male domination.

- Finally, one of the most important reasons why child sex exploitation is taking place among tourists is because the children are readily available. The ease with which tourists in some countries can obtain a child as a sexual partner is, in itself, a powerful incentive for some to try the novelty of a child sex partner. The role of organised crime in the supply of children must be recognised. Because tourists are often willing to pay large sums of money for sexual services from children, the trade in children has become more lucrative to criminals and therefore more commonplace.

What are Prostitution and Sex Tourism?

Prostitution and sex tourism fall under a more general category of sexual exploitation. Sexual exploitation happens when one person (or persons) receives sex or money through abusing another person's sexuality.

For an example of prostitution, a man may receive sex and a pimp may receive money by using a woman as a prostitute. In sex tourism, an American man may pay a sex travel agency for a trip to Thailand which includes air-fare, hotel, food, and women for sex. Prostitution can include traditional forms of prostitution (through a brothel, the military, or on the streets), and also sex tourism, sex trafficking, and mail order bride selling.

Who is Affected by Prostitution and Sex Tourism?

It is difficult to estimate how many people are working in prostitution because so many women working as waitresses, hotel maids, sales-clerks, bar girls, and golf caddies are forced into prostitution as part of their work, In Thailand, it has been estimated that at least 200,000 women and children work in prostitution. At least one-third of Thai prostitutes are under the age of 18, and most adult prostitutes started when they were only children. Children as young as six years old work in prostitution. Prostitutes are primarily women and girls, although some men and boys also work in prostitution.

Many of the children who work in prostitution come from extremely poor families—the child's work as a prostitute may feed her entire family. Women and children may also be illegal trafficked from one country to another under the belief that they will find work in another country. Their traffickers force them to pay a high price, and to work in prostitution on their arrivals in order to pay for their travel.

How are People Working to Solve the Problem of Prostitution and Sex Tourism?

• *Criminalizing Prostitution*

Although prostitution is illegal in Thailand, it is often protected by law enforcement agencies. When prostitution is illegal, it often means that it is illegal for a woman to be a prostitute, but not illegal for a man to pay a prostitute. This continues to harm the woman who is in prostitution, instead of helping her find ways out of prostitution. It also gives men free license to continue to find other women to exploit. When making prostitution illegal, the roles should be switched; men should be arrested for purchasing a prostitute, while women should not be thrown in jail for being a prostitute.

• *Promoting Policies that Address Prostitution*

Governments have a role in prosecuting companies that sell sex tourist packages. For example, in New York, prostitution laws state that: "a person is guilty of promoting prostitution in the third degree when he knowingly advances or profits from prostitution by managing, supervising, controlling or owning...a prostitution business or enterprise involving prostitution activity by two or more prostitutes...." Sex tourism agencies originating in New York could be prosecuted under this law.

The World Bank has a role in addressing prostitution when it is loaning $1.9 billion US dollars to Thailand for projects. Its *history* of supporting sex tourism in Thailand makes it unlikely that current policy critically considers the effects of sex tourism on women in children. In fact, the

Current World Bank pages on Thailand do not even mention the sex tourism industry or prostitution. Projects to improve the lives of women and children in Thailand cannot work if the role of sex tourism is not addressed.

• *Increasing Opportunities in Education and Employment*

Women and children are not freely choosing the work in prostitution; it is a "choice" based purely on the economics of food and shelter. Girls who work as prostitutes in Thailand can provide for their entire family, while most other jobs cannot. It will take economic change to help women and children seriously considering leaving the sex tourism industry. Jobs must be available that can provide for families, and people must be trained to do them. New industry must replace the current sex industry to enact real change for women and children in prostitution.

International tourism is one of the word's largest "industries" and it has grown rapidly during the last forty years. It's rapid expansion and spread to many countries as a key way of earning valuable foreign exchange to boost economic growth has generated numerous problems for countries, regions and cities and especially in the poorer countries. These include the following: environmental devastation, economic dependency on low wage service jobs and the leaking of tourist earning back to the rich countries because it is their huge companies which mostly supply the loans for tourists development, the transport facilities (airlines), imported foods, hotel investments etc.

International tourism also has important implications for society, culture and issues of national identity. For example, how far are authentic "traditional" practices, rituals, beliefs and forms of social organization—the authority of the elders over the young, gender relations etc.—undermined or even lost as a consequence of the arrival of wealthy foreign visitors many of whom demand resort facilities, western-quality amenities and who engage in hedonistic pursuits?

In this project, however, we explore one of the problems created by international tourism: the rise of sex tourism and the world wide efforts to counter it and its ill effects. Although the exploitation by certain kinds of tourists of young women has always been prominent, especially in South East Asia the "trade" in young children of both sexes for sexual exploitation has also grown considerably in recent years. This project concentrates on the latter aspect of sex tourism:

1. How extensive is the problem of child sex tourism?
2. What are the main causes of child sex tourism and why has its incidence increased so much? How would you evaluate the relative importance of these causes? Why is that successful economic development in some less developed countries and the general raising of living standards does not seem to make an impact on this evil trade so that it continues to increase?
3. What have been some of the main international responses to this problem and what initiatives are under way to deal with it

How do Prostitution and Sex Tourism Affect Health?

- ***Physical Health***

The sexual health of women and children in prostitution is severely harmed in many ways:

- Increased risk of HIV/AIDS
- Risk of sexually transmitted infections
- Risk of unwanted pregnancy
- Vaginal tearing

- Violence
- Rape
- Physical abuse
- Confinement.

• ***Mental Health***

Prostitution is a violation of women's human rights, and treats women as objects. The pain of being treated so poorly can lead to depression and resignation. The state of girls' mental health is best illustrated by Poppy, quoted in *The Child and the Tourist* by Ron O'Grady:

"I found myself dancing at a club at the age of 11.... I have had different kinds of customers, foreigners and Filipinos. I tried suicide but it didn't work so I turned to drugs. I want to die before my next birthday."

• ***Women's Health***

Prostitution teaches men to view women as objects. Thus not only are women and children who are prostitutes harmed, but **all** women are harmed by prostitution.

Why do Prostitution and Sex Tourism Affect Third World Women More Than Others?

Prostitution has become an industry in Thailand with the major help of the United States military and the World Bank. During the Vietnam War, the U.S. Department of Defence had a contract with the Thai Government to provide "Recreation and Relaxation" for U.S. soldiers. With money from the U.S. Government, local Thai prostitution organized and expanded into a major industry. In 1975, the World Bank built an economic plan for Thailand around the sex tourism industry, which helped turn sex tourism into the country's number one export." Prostitution has now become such an important industry, that work to end prostitution must also support the growth of new industries.

ABOUT CHILD SEX TOURISM

Comprehending Child Sex Tourism

To many Governments around the world, international tourism provides an answer to economic growth and development. As tourism begins to overtake traditional sources of employment, children and young people are encouraged to migrate to tourism areas, in hopes they can earn an income for themselves and their families.

The commercial sexual exploitation of children parallels the growth of tourism many parts of the world. Tourism is not the cause of child sexual exploitation, but it does provide easy access to vulnerable children. In some instances, the marketing of certain destinations, particularly within Asia, portrays an image of women and children who are passive, submissive and exotic. These false images reinforce many of the beliefs of sex tourists.

Tourism also brings consumerism to many parts of the world previously denied access to luxury commodities and services. The lure of this easy money has caused many young people, including children, to trade their bodies in exchange for T-shirts, walkmans, bikes and even air tickets out of the country. In other situations, children are trafficked into the brothels on the margins of the tourist area and sold into sexual slavery, very rarely earning the money to escape.

Profiles

Sex tourists may be solo travellers or part of an arranged group. They may be Preferential Abusers, who have clear and definite sexual preferences for children or Situational Abusers, offenders who may not have planned to have commercial child sex while abroad, but took the opportunity when it presented itself. They use the "why not" approach and might consider it a bit of holiday "fun" not considering adolescents as children, even though many of the bar girls and boys are under 16 years of age.

While the majority of child sex offenders are male, it is also known that women are involved, and in some cases, male and female offenders travel as a couple to avoid discovery. Child sex tourist persuade themselves that in another country, normal social and moral restraints can be discarded, along with the belief that one will not be held responsible for his or her behaviour. It is within these circumstances that child sexual exploitation thrives.

The fact that most organized international child sex abuse occurs in developing countries indicates that child sex offenders exploit the economic hardships which many families endure. Offenders prefer to believe that the children they abuse are professional prostitutes, which allow the perpetrators to feel exonerated or justified in their actions. The fear of contracting AIDS through unprotected sex with older prostitutes has increased the demand for virgins and young children.

WHY IS THIS HAPPENING TO WOMEN AND CHILDREN?

- Devaluation of the girl child and discriminatory practices
- Perceived responsibility of women and children to support families
- Lack of educational, employment and vocational opportunities
- Fragmentation of families: death of parent/s, husband, increases homeless women and children
- Economic conditions, especially rural poverty, fuelled

by economic development policies and the erosion of agricultural sectors

- Rural to urban migration and the growth of urban industrial centers
- Move from subsistence to cash based economy and increased consumerism
- Lack of laws and law enforcement.

Demand

- Criminal networks who organize the sex industry and recruit the children
- Law enforcement /Governmental complicity in the sex trade
- Demands of foreign sex industries creating international trade in girls and women
- Fear of AIDS, leading customers to demand younger girls
- Early marriage and child marriage
- Traditional and cultural practices, including the demand for virgins, the cultural practice of men patronizing prostitutes, inter-generational patterns of girls entering prostitution
- Employers using the debt-bond (slavery) system, forced labour and child labour
- Demand of sex tourists, pedophiles and the migrant labour force
- International promotion of the sex industry through information technology.

International tourism organisations have been unanimous in condemning the use of tourism for the commercial sexual exploitation of children. The World Tourism Organisation calls it a .violation of the Convention on the Rights of the Child which requires strict legal action by tourist sending and receiving countries. (Oct. 22, 1995). The Universal Federation of Travel Agents. Associations, one of the first travel organisations to condemn child prostitution, has produced a Children.s and Travel Agents. Charter which is being circulated for signature by national members and which pledges to "give every assistance to the various organisations, campaigns and charitable associations concerned with the welfare of child victims of sex tourism to help restore the dignity, physical and mental health to such children". It is appropriate that the Congress in Sweden should recognise the growing concern among tourism bodies about the situation of children in prostitution and the related issues of sex tourism. Current estimates put the number of children entering the sex-market every year at well above one million. This issue is now being widely discussed within the industry itself and it is hoped that a new consensus will emerge from the Congress on how the tourism industry can help the international community bring an end to this modern form of slavery. This paper provides the background to the involvement of the tourism industry with the issue and describes some of the actions which have been taken. Many people have contributed to the preparation and drafting of this paper. Officials from the World Tourism Organization (WTO), the Universal Federation of Travel Agents' Associations (UFTAA), the International Air Transport Association (IATA) and the International Union of Food, Agriculture, Hotel, Restaurant, Catering, Tobacco and Allied Workers. Associations (IUF) have been particularly helpful.

Sex Tourism involves tourists traveling from a economically wealthy country to a poorer one (and one with usually less strict morality laws) for the purpose of engaging in sex with prostitutes. Common destinations for sex tourists include Thailand, Brazil, Cambodia, and Costa Rica. Since the collapse of the Iron Curtain, Russia and the Czech Republic have also become popular destinations for sex tourists.

While the overwhelming majority of sex tourists only engage in this activity with other adults, a very small percentage actively look for underage child prostitutes. Several countries have severe laws on the books making sex with children (see paedophilia) abroad a serious offence.

WHAT IS SEX TOURISM?

I believe that a materialistic and biological approach is appropriate for most philosophical issues. "Materialistic" in this context does not mean: based on financial considerations. Rather, "materialistic" denotes a philosophical school that basically adheres to the assessment that everything that is has a cause, and the cause is in the material world. The antonym to materialistic is idealistic. As a philosophical category, the term "idealistic" denotes that people believe that what exists in this world has its causes in the realm of an invisible force that has no material representation in this world. For example, those who believe that man has been created by a god, and that there is a parallel world, named heaven, would be classified as idealists.

In a more narrow, everyday sense, those who adhere to a materialistic philosophy are more likely than idealists to see down-to-earth causal connections for what exists, and for what we do. Idealists would believe that a person's actions are guided by his moral values, while materialists would assume that practical interests guide these actions.

What a "biological approach" means is more directly understood. We, members of the species homo sapiens, are primates, closely related to apes, and some very-very basic biological axioms apply to us, just as they apply to chimps or orangutans.

Basic axioms that apply not just to the higher mammals but to all animals are: we all aim to avoid (as best as one can) losing one's life, seek nutrition, and pursue sexual satisfaction and procreation. Like a mathematician who reduces a meter-long equation into something as simple as Pythagoras' formula all expressions of human life somehow fall into the above-mentioned categories.

Why then, does our civilization seem so complicated? Actually, from my materialistic and biological perspective, it appears much less complicated than politicians, ideologues, writers, and philosophers make us believe. Much of what we consider culture, from a biological point of view, has about the same value as a rooster's comb.

This is not a book on the pros and cons of a materialistic and biological view of life. It is an article on sex tourism.

I do not intend to involve myself in the debate on the degree to which sex tourism is deplorable. I generally do not think in moral categories. They are too arbitrary, and apart from that, they are tainted by a lot of hypocrisy and hype.

I actually believe that sex tourism is a natural social phenomenon. If we assume that striving for sexual satisfaction is a primary motivator in people's life, than it is understandable if men hunt where they can find easier prey.

This article is not politically correct. I am not interested in political correctness. I am interested only in the truth.

They can legislate equal rights for men and women. That's fine with me. But this doesn't alter some very basic points of mammalian biology. The sexual relationships of mammalians aren't as exclusive as the sexual relationships of birds. Among practically all mammalians, dominant men strive for sexual access to a good number of females. Even when strong one-on-one partnerships are formed, every opportunity for a sexual encounter with a new partner is appreciated.

This is neither in accordance with accepted moral standards, nor is it politically correct. But it's still the pattern beneath even formal behaviour. A commander-in-chief may make a decision to go to war because less for political reasons but because it affords him the opportunity to be away from home with a mistress. Or an Australian diplomat may pursue a posting in Cambodia because child sex is much easier arranged there than, for example, in Canada.

Men have a natural interest in building sort-of-harems, which, in our days, means: maintaining multiple parallel sexual relationships. And if the chances to achieve such a setting are slim in Europe or the US, or if such an undertaking requires undue effort, they will move to more favourable grounds.

North Americans and Europeans have an easy time setting up multiple sexual relationships in South America, in many countries in Asia, and in Africa. And they usually can pick the most attractive girls.

This behaviour can be regulated, but as long as the basis on which it grows is not withdrawn, it cannot be rooted out.

The basis is that for as long as in Third World countries, the sexual interests of North American and European men are a perfect match for the feeding (economic) interests of local women and girls, the business of matchmakers will thrive.

I believe that it is a natural phenomenon that men are guided by interests of sexual conquests, and women by concerns of protection and feeding (apart from less pronounced sexual interests).

We should stop to see ourselves as fundamentally different from other primates. We are just apes who have developed a more sophisticated system of communication (a.k.a. language), and therefore the means to accumulate technological advancement throughout generations, and to share results with a large number of other members of our species.

But down below, we are just apes. Our basic motivations are animal-like: to avoid the destruction of our individual life, to seek nutrition, and to pursue sexual satisfaction. So-called higher values are usually fake.

Or rather, we can easily unveil the materialistic, biological forces behind the facade.

People don't take action in order to implement moral notions, or political correctness. They take action because it matches their interests. Only after having decided for a certain course, they take action to veil the interests behind their decisions and pretend to become active out of adherence to moral imperatives, which is easier to sell to the public than self-interest. It's wise tactics to behave like this.

It doesn't matter that often, people are not even aware that they pursue goals because they match their interests, and instead believe themselves that they do it out of virtue. To behave in accordance to one's interests does not require awareness. Natural selection assures that only those whose behaviour matches their interests will procreate.

If we take the phenomenon of sex tourism, we will see that the approach taken by each and every social groups is in tune with their biological interests.

Western male sex tourists usually find nothing wrong with their behaviour, or at least they claim that what is wrong is none of their business. They frequent cheap local prostitutes, marry attractive local women, and play around in other modes.

Young local women who derive material benefit from the sex tourists also find nothing wrong with it. They need the source of income... for themselves, and for their offspring.

In both cases, the opinion they subscribe to matches their biological interests.

Now to the coalition of those who oppose sex tourism, allegedly out of moral concern.

The women in the countries from where male sex tourists hail are usually strongly against sex tourism. No wonder. Their biological interest is that "their" men stay at home and compete for the females of their own societies... and do not go abroad for easier, younger, and more attractive women. They have reason to be jealous. The women sought by male sex tourists in Third World countries are their immediate competitors.

They may love their men, and hate their female competitors, but this will not be the issue they publicly address. Publicly, they deplore the exploitive character of the relationships of Western sex tourists in Third World countries. When sex tourism issues are discussed anywhere in the world, I know ahead the position occupied by representatives of Western womanhood. No sympathy with sex tourists!

And in order to provide substance to their cause, they will lobby Third World Governments to implement specific laws pertaining to the sexual conduct of foreign men.

I know already their coalition partners: the local men in Third World countries. How could they possibly accept happily the presence of Western men who prey on their girls and women? The local men themselves want to prey on their girls and women. Western men are unwelcome competitors; all the more as Western men usually have a substantial economic edge.

It is no surprise that young women in Third World countries dream of husbands from North America or Europe. They may even be able to migrate from the Third World to the Old World (Europe) or the New World (the Americas). A heaven of social and financial security awaits them. The anti-coalition, of course, is much stronger than the coalition of those who benefit from a sex tourism constellation. Therefore, we can see the conditions becoming worse for sex tourists anywhere in the world, at least in peacetime.

But enter war and destruction, terrorism and natural disasters, anything that erodes social order. Then you have a new playing ground for men from rich societies hunting for sexual gratification among the poor women in a newly or once again poor country. For when they are down, the sex tourists are up. Local men in Third World countries can't offer such prospects. Therefore, they hate Western sex tourists and want girls who condole with them severely punished. (Mentally, gang rape by angry local men would be the preferred punishment, but in our times, such measures are difficult to implement in many countries, at least in peacetime.)

Somebody missing in the anti-coalition? Oh yes, of course: elder local women in Third World countries (at least those who's daughters aren't about to marry Western men, thus providing an emigration route for the whole family).

With predictable accuracy, all social strata involved propagate opinions that are in accordance with their biological interests. This cannot be an accident. It's their being part of, and member in, a specific social group, which determines the opinion they subscribe to; they do not arrive at specific opinions out of moral consideration, or concerns of human rights.

PROSTITUTION IN SEX TOURISM

The sexual exploitation of girls and boys, largely by men from the United States, has reached alarming proportions in Central America, according to children's rights advocates who say the region is now a priority in their struggle against child prostitution and pornography.

A major reason for growth in the Central American child-sex trade, children's advocates say, is that traditional desti-nations for such activity—chiefly. Thailand and the Philippines—have blunted the sex tourism business over the last two years by enacting public awareness campaigns and stricter laws and enforcement measures.

Prostitution among the children who live and work on the streets of Latin America—their number has been estimated, at up to 40 million—has long been a consequence of the region's poverty. But as such countries as Guatemala, El Salvador, Costa Rica and Nicaragua step up efforts to promote their beaches, volcanoes and natural beauty as tourist destinations, they attract greater numbers of men from North America, Europe and other Latin American countries looking for sex with children.

"What we are seeing is the dark side of tourism," said, Heimo Laakkonen, head of UNICEF in Costa Rica. Mr. Laakkonen said that while sexual exploitation of minors is not a new problem in the region, the problem has gotten worse with the increase in tourism. Children's rights activists have accused Governments in Central America, where about 54 per cent of the population is below the age of 18, of being slow to confront the burgeoning child prostitution and pornography industry.

"It involves a certain level of political maturity on the part of Governments to acknowledge the severity of the problem, as opposed to the ostrich syndrome of keeping your head stuck in the sand," said Bruce Harris, regional director of Covenant House Latin America, an organization that helps street children.

Although there are no statistics to quantify the scope of sexual exploitation of children in Central America, anecdotal evidence, independent surveys and a string of recent arrests of North Americans—as well as of other foreigners and locals—support the contention that the problem is growing.

The increased demand for child prostitutes in this region and others stems partly from the mistaken impression that older prostitutes are more likely than younger ones to have AIDS or carry HIV virus, experts say.

Carlos Roverssi, former executive president of the National Child Trust, the Costa Rican child welfare agency, acknowledged last year that there had been an accelerated increase in child prostitution in the country, which he said was largely the result of the unofficial promotion of sex tourism in Costa Rica over the Internet.

In Nicaragua, a recent UNICEF report said, there has been significant growth in the prostitution of children between the ages of 12 and 16 in towns where taxi drivers were reported to serve as middlemen.

Several months ago, agents of the International Police Organization Interpol operating out of El Salvador discovered a prostitution network that was trafficking young girls from several countries in Central America to work in bars along the border of El Salvador and Guatemala.

Interpol also said that it had rescued about 20 Salvadoran girls from such prostitution and pornography industry from prostitution rings during the past three years and, it involves a certain level of political links.

SUCCESS IN BATTLE AGAINST SEX TOURISM

Second World Congress place in Yokohama, Japan in December 2001. Governments asked to renew and extend the commitments they made at the first meeting. An encouraging case study-curbing sex tourism: Many 'sex tourists' deliberately travel abroad to have sex with children because they believe it is legal and culturally acceptable. But there is also hope in the fact that advocates like ECPAT have succeeded in engaging airlines, Governments, and travel agencies in their work.

By 1995, international travel trade associations representing hotels and restaurants, travel agents and airlines had all passed resolutions condemning child sex tourism. In 1996, the World Tourism Organization established Child Prostitution and Tourism Watch, a task force involving the tourism industry, Governments and NGOs to campaign against this terrible scourge.

Governments started to join in. The ministry of tourism in Brazil launched a very effective poster campaign. The Australian Government distributed thousands of brochures advertising the laws against child sex tourism as a deterrent. Until now, no US airline has agreed to join the video campaign, in spite of appeals from NGOs, the President of Air France and the U.S. Department of Transportation.

Prevention: In an important project, ECPAT is currently working with five local organizations to prevent young people from entering the commercial sex industry in Northern Thailand. The project is funded by Taksvarkkiry Dagsvereke of Finland, and the results are promising.

More and more communities in Northern Thailand are aware of the dangers. More children are aware of their rights and are starting to enforce them. No child followed by the partners as part of the Taksvarkki project has entered the sex trade, and the small number that have left their communities for work stay in contact with their relatives.

In France, the Government and travel associations adapted the syllabus for tourism schools to include information about child sex tourism. In France, Germany, Belgium and the Netherlands a luggage tag condemning child sex tourism has been made widely available. In Italy a similar high-profile campaign has gone forward with partners in Government and the travel industry.

Tour operators in Europe and elsewhere in Europe are signing on to a code of conduct against child sex tourism, and Asian tour operators are receiving training in how to deal with the issue of child sex tourism when they are confronted with it. In the United States, the American Society of Travel Agents has signed on to the no-child-sex tourism campaign.

Among airlines, Air France has led the way by producing an in-flight video in conjunction with ECPAT that was shown on all long-haul fights. Lufthansa has also produced a n in-flight video against child sex tourism. Now eleven European airlines (including Alitalia, Swiss Air, Finnair and Sabena) also show these in-flight videos.

2

LEGALIZATION AND ERADICATION OF PROSTITUTION

The subject of women reveals a consensus that society's focus was constantly on the changes and reform that was expected of these women, but in contrasts, the reality was that it was society's responses and attitudes that has to change drastically if at all these women had to be helped. This journey took me from the narrow streets of Banaras, through Orissa, Andhra Pradesh, Karnataka, Maharashtra, Uttar Pradesh, Madhya Pradesh, Manipur, Sikkim, Assam, Goa, West Bengal, Bihar and Kerala where I met more than 80,000 women in various situations and circumstances and heard them speak "openly, without fear, and with hope".

Throughout my discussions with various women and children the foremost request was that they should be treated as equal citizens of India. I also agreed that we do not want the traditional *soft options* for these women. I strongly felt that their requirements and concerns be set out firmly in all the developmental issues.

During those discussions I recognised the major role and value of collectivism and the building of cooperative self-help spirit and institution among the women in prostitution. This we found to be an important first step towards change both for themselves and the violence within the societies which contain and perpetuate these systems.

Although the wisdom of Chanakya can be related here calling this profession an "invisible profession", an attempt has been made nowadays to make this group of women visible. The question is would this visibility jeopardize their existence ?

I personally chose to hear these thousands of voices in the hope of evoking appropriate responses and capture the landscape of prostitution in the country in the hope of analysing the issue. Hence today the hottest debate among women's groups is whether to legalize this profession or not. Today most of the women activists seek answers to this question in meetings, seminars, conventions and national consultations.

During all my visits to the various meetings in the red light areas I asked the women, "Daughter, what is it you want"? And in each of these meeting the answers were always "Ma, I don't want my daughter to be in this profession. Please take here away and keep her in a boarding school". Hence I do believe that no prostitute really thinks that this could be a dignified profession for her child—and leads me to conclude that really speaking they would not like legalization.

Article 19(1) (g) of the Constitution says : "All citizens shall have the right to practise any profession, or to carry on any occupation, trade or business." And in Article 21 : "No person shall be deprived of his life or personal liberty except according to procedure established by law. "The group demanding legalization quotes from the above two Articles and calls upon the fundamental rights of every citizen to practise any profession he/she may choose.

The most vocal among groups advertising legalization of prostitution is the Mahila Samanwaya Committee, Calcutta. They held two conferences of the National Network of Sex Workers at Salt Lake Stadium in Calcutta in March,

1998 perhaps it was for the first time that the sports stadium hosted a conference on prostitution. It was attached by 1600 sex workers including 12 delegates of the Asia-Pacific Network of Sex Workers. The conference *inter alia* discussed issues like depcriminalisation of prostitution through repeal of the Prevention of Immoral Traffic Act, legal recognition of trade and of sex workers as workers and their right to form a trade union, a self-regulatory board to allow sex workers to gain control over their own work and also to prevent entry of minor girls into flesh trade. The sex workers declared that they earned their bread from manual work and as such wanted to be recognised as industrial labourers. They did not want any more girls to be tricked into the profession.

It was generally felt that sex workers still remain outcasts and untouchables according to conventional morality. They were even denied the attention that slum dwellers received. It was time now that they were freed of the long-time ignominy heaped upon them. Legalisation of sex workers would help contain child prostitution, forced prostitution, Devadasi system besides reducing atrocities at the hands of mafia and police and as also would help maintain their health.

During the conference several resolutions were passed and at the end of the conference the sex workers' organisations decided to approach MPs to get their profession recognised. They also wanted favourable material to be prepared to put up a case for the sex workers' rights. A public opinion survey conducted during the Calcutta Book Fair, 1988 held from 28th January to 8th February, 1998, in which 525 persons most of them educated, responded, was also released. It revealed that over 80 percent of those who responded accepted that the profession should be legalised and sex workers must also enjoy equal rights. Seventy three percent of the responder's opined that children of sex workers should be known by their mother's identity. About the motive behind police raids, a large section of the respondents (72.6 percent) opined that police conducted raids primarily to harass the sex workers as it was the easiest way for the police to extort money.

At a national meeting of the National Commission for Women held at Delhi in 1996 an idea to form a collective to safeguard the interests of women in prostitution was mooted. While the concept of such collectives is in its infancy in India, the women who are its members are learning how to negotiate with society and earn a dignified place for themselves. Shabana from Nippani is part of VAMP or Veshya AIDS Muqabla Parishad which is a collective of women in prostitution. She said, "Now that we women can work on our, we shall ourselves solve our problems instead of running to someone else. Our collective gives us a powerful identity as also the means to fight the problems connected with sex work and we are gaining in confidence."

At first they could not believe that they could come together as a result of a collective which was formed in 1996. The Chittoor Mahila AIDS control Sangham (CMACS) was registered as a collective of sex workers with the aim of promoting the health and welfare of women. This organisation has given tremendous confidence and strength to the women. In some cases, the need for collective has stemmed from dissatisfaction with the NGOs working with women in prostitution. It was felt that the NGOs were representing their own interests and not those of the women they were working for. Lata was deserted by her husband when she was sixteen and later sold into a Mumbai brothel. She says: "We do not need NGOs to speak on our behalf they are a big problem. We are doing real social work ourselves, interacting with the community, spreading awareness about AIDS, distributing condom, conducting health programmes and releasing women from unlawful custody."

It was felt that the presence of a self-regulatory board would go a long way in solving the problem. It should be constituted with a specified number of sex workers and non-sex workers—professionals like doctors, legal experts, etc. This board should control the trade. The advantages of such a board, the participants felt, would be:

(a) Forcing women into the trade would be restricted.

(b) The middlemen would not be able to demand large kickbacks.

(c) One would enter the trade with a fuller knowledge of it.

(d) The board could deal with grievances particularly those arising out of members of police and medical community.

(e) A model code of conduct could be laid down by the board.

(f) Such a board will be effective in preventing the entry of underage girls in the trade.

(g) The board can make the use of condoms mandatory.

(h) A recognised profession and a recognised trade will protect from exploitation by police.

(i) The self–regulatory board will be the first stepping stone in the sex worker's quest for more rights. The board will be a symbol of the legitimacy of their lives.

(j) Sex workers will have more control over their bodies if they have a board and can say 'no' to a client.

(k) The board will help to shield them from protection

rackets run by landlords the police and local thugs.

The group demanding legalization was of view that this will lead to acceptance of reality, will bring some rules and regulation for this section of women and will protect and safeguard them. Once legalized, the business of prostitution may be monitored and will discipline the defaulting houses. If legalized, the brothels could be isolated as an authorized place where whoever wants to utilize the services of a prostitute can do so without involvement of any middlemen. This group of activists believes that legalization will eliminate the involvement of pimps, brothelkeepers, madams, and traffickers. The woman practising prostitution will not be obliged to part with her income to this group of people who at present snatch a lion's share from her earnings. On the other hand, consequently, legalization will also reduce racketeering and forcing of minors into this vortex. The girls will no longer remain in the clutches of crime perpetuators nor will forever be bound to repay the "debt" they have not taken. Laws, thus enacted, would enable every woman practising prostitution to move the court if being bullied, assaulted, harassed or coerced by anti-social elements, pimps clients or even police. If given a licence, all prostitutes could come together under the same umbrella and may form a union like any other to look after their rights. Their status as bonded labour will vanish.

Today, old as well as sick women are thrown out of brothels and have no place to go. Their families refuse to accept them, the government has no provision for such women anywhere and ultimately they go back to the profession and operate independently. Activists believe the important turn in their situation would be that they will have free access to medical services. Then, they will not sell their sick and tainted bodies to earn their livelihood. And, rehabilitation centres would be run and it would become obligatory to tend for old and sick sex workers in their difficult times.

Another section of women activists oppose the above arguments and are against legalization. Unlike as in the West, in our Indian society our culture, traditions and moral values taboo sex in the open or even talking about it in normal discussions among family members and even among friends. In Western countries, child-parent relationship is not as strong and so individuals, while growing up and during adolescence, seek emotional security and dependency among their peer groups or even elders resulting in weak and unstable relationship between boys and girls and subsequently men and women. This leads to free open sex in the society and is very well accepted. But the same is not true in our country. Of course, the mentality of the younger generation along with moral values are fast changing in India but still the things are under the control of elders. People are more inclined to copy Western culture but at the same time they are not able to leave the Indian traditions behind absolutely. No doubt, though prostitution is a reality but it is accepted as a social evil.

Even if legalized, the women practising the trade will never be able to shake off the label and stigma of prostitution attached to them. Our society will still not accept them in mainstream. Even in the West, women with the label of prostitutes are not considered fit for the mainstream. The reason lies in the fact that prostitution is a clandestine profession and violative of the laws of society as well as of the country.

The group of women activists against legalization consider prostitution bad for the physical, mental, social and moral health of an individual and consequently of society. On the contrary, there is a widespread opinion of some educators and for matters of society that "prostitution acts as a sewage system for extra-seminal fluid in the society." The society is cleansed of the evil of rape and other sexual offences because of the existence of prostitution. It is ironical that in today's environment when more and more individuals, especially children are being pushed into this trade each day to make prostitution legal, as it is now "a five billion dollar" industry, there is tremendous increase in sexual offences especially incest and rape of minors. At this rate where are we heading to? With both graphs showing consistent increase, will legalizing prostitution help reduce the agony of poor, vulnerable women and children? And the most important question currently being asked is will legalisation of the sex trade solve the problem of children? It is a general feeling that legalization will result in business being carried on both legally and illegally.

Do we give licence to smugglers, thieves and anti-social elements to do their job. If they start asking for licence to carry out their respective jobs which are equally illegal, will some of the other organization support them, ever. Then why should prostitution be legalized? Legalization would vitiate the moral atmosphere of the country. It would give anti social elements the licence to indulge in trafficking and trade of humans. Do we legalize corruption? If we could legalize corruption we could a well legalize-prostitution.

The group of women in favour of legalization hold the believe that it will reduce the incidence of HIV/AIDS and will act as a preventive measure for the spread of dreadful diseases as the women will have full rights and would be able to insist on safe sex. If the client does not agree she would have full right to turn him out. This seems very ideal but the example of Australia tells us otherwise.

When prostitution was legalized in Australia to obtain a licence the women needed to have mandatory testing for HIV and certificate for disease-free body. An impact on society was felt as a large number of clients were attracted to legalized brothels. This practice, instead of preventing or reducing the spread of disease, led to increase in the number of HIV cases as it was customers who spread the disease than the prostitutes.

Many case-studies have been cited in the next few chapters where it is seen that young girls are introduced to the clients as virgins at a tender age. At the time of induction they are healthy but in about two years' time they are cases of full-blown dreadful diseases as STDs, tuberculosis, HIV/AIDS, etc. Who is responsible for their such condition? Again, it has happened because they are exposed to a large number of clients and have no right to insist on safe sex. In this condition either these girls are dumped or thrown out of the brothels with nowhere else to go. Will legalization solve the problem of such women?

Based on the discussions, and the conclusions therefrom, the following points can be suggested as recommendations However, it should be noted that these recommendations have been formulated on the assumption that flesh trade and trafficking are not the same and flesh trade cannot be wiped out form society while trafficking can be done away with. Regardless of all constraining measures, there will always be some persons who would largely depend on the flesh trade markets satisfying their carnal desires even if it may be just for fun and involve money spending and money earned.

Abolition of the trade to a considerable degree is a long term goal, whereas prevention and control are processes yielding result if taken up in right earnest, and involvement, Mobilisation and participation of the people however, forms the key to both.

To make an effective impact on the problem as it exists today, steps will have to be taken firstly to prevent new entrants into flesh trade, and secondly, to rescue and rehabilitate those girl/ women who are unwilling functionaries of the trade. For checking further entry of new girls/women into flesh trade, the following suggestions should be taken into consideration.

(A) *Initiating integrated and comprehensive rural development programme specially for women* for the prone areas in terms of original place of residence of the victims and others which are inhabited by castes/communities with traditional acceptance of flesh trade. The objectives of this development programme would be:

(i) to increase awareness, literacy rate and educational standard and imparting skills. Efforts to increase awareness for change of attitude of the people would not be confined to the victim alone. It should aim at covering the society as a whole in phases starting within the family. This awareness building process should also emphasise on the mechanism of operation of the trade and its consequences on the victims and their families.

(ii) to provide alternative employment facilities.

(iii) to improve health, nutrition, sanitation and recreation facilities.

(B) *Alongwith rural development, proper urban development and town planning programmes have to be organised.* Family Housing Scheme, sanitation and recreation facilities should be the focal points of these plans and programmes. Proper housing facilities should be emphasised upon to minimize the number of men staying away from their families, who are potential clients in the flesh trade markets. Special attention must be paid to the housing problems of the industrial and other workers, migrant workers, police and armed forces personnel.

Once these rural and urban development programmes are implemented in right interest, new entrants into the trade on the grounds of illiteracy, ignorance, poverty, unemployment, absence of proper recreational facilities and housing, lack of parental care, etc. would be automatically reduced.

In order to strengthen the effort and hasten the process of prevention, it may be necessary to bind the traditional castes/communities by some legislation like the Naik Girls Protection Act 1929, which aims to prevent the Naik girls from becoming prostitutes. Such an Act must also include within its purview those traditional practices lead to and promote flesh trade.

(C) *Despite all these efforts, functionaries of the trade are likely to persist with their attempts to trap girls/women for induction into the trade.* To checkmate such attempts the following steps should be taken:

(i) ensure strict vigilance and instill administrative will among concerned persons to make effective use of the existing laws.

(ii) police role being of vital importance in making use of existing laws, the police personnel should be made aware of the sufferings of the victims, and the unsocial activities of those in the trade, this would require proper orientation of the policemen towards this problem.

(iii) consolidate the position of the Rescue Officer and define his role and responsibilities in manner that he can contribute towards ameliorating the problem.

(iv) Groups of social workers with police support should be authorised to identify those victims who want to be removed from the red light areas.

(v) Investigate the credentials of persons offering bail, and those who claim to be related to the victim.

(vi) Police and administrative functionaries are found to be patronising the trade in any capacity, and neglecting their duty with regard to the enforcement of laws, or indulging in exploitation of women to be severely punished.

(vii) Provide legal aid to victims of the trade for which, legal aid cells should be activated to take up such cases on priority basis; where no legal aid facilities are available, new legal aid cells should be formed.

(viii) Formation of some monitoring agency by the government with legal authority to take actions based on its observation to monitor the implementation of the laws pertaining to flesh trade and trafficking including licensing and regulation of the practice of the trade. Such agency should include prominent persons genuinely concerned about the problem and its implications.

(D) *The possibility of voluntary involvement of girls/ women in flesh trade cannot be ruled out.* In such cases licensing and regulation should be resorted to keeping in mind the following suggestions:

(a) Prostitution without valid licence should be a punishable offence, as also violation of licence rules.

(b) The licensing authority must have the details of the women applying for a licence like her age, present address, permanent address proposed place of business, name of landlord and also the present occupant, in case the landlord is not the occupant of proposed place of business, etc. along with her recent photograph (to be renewed after every five years).

(c) The licence should be valid for a period of one year only, at a time. During the validity of the licence the woman will be subject to intermittent health checks. If she is found afflicted with STO, her licence should be withheld till she is completely cured.

(d) Applications for licence must be accompanied by a medical fitness issued by an authorised medical practitioner.

(e) Wherever she may live, the women should be allowed to practice only in the prescribed area, but not close to public places.

(f) The licence should be non-transferable.

(E) *The rehabilitation programme through the Protective Homes* as at present is inadequate. The following suggestions are made to make it more effective:

(a) The Home should be used for the prescribed purpose only. Followup should form an integral part of activities of every Home.

(b) The staff of the Home should receive proper training and guidance., wherever possible the staff should be multilingual to deal effectively with the inmates belonging to different regions.

(c) There should be a board of advisors presided over by the District Magistrate/Eminent Social workers attached to each Home. Members should be expected to visit the home at least once every year and send reports of their visits to the D.M. Through the Social Welfare Officer.

(d) Every effort has to be made to establish family contacts to promote rehabilitation of the victims. For this purpose, arrangements have to be made either to make visits or to contact the family by using various sources, where rehabilitation is not done through family, then efforts must be made for rehabilitation through self-employment and marriage.

(e) Voluntary agencies and selected individuals should be involved in counselling and for imparting skills.

(f) A properly trained inmate should be eligible for government aid to set up own business. Such cases may be linked up with IRDP and SWCRA, TRYSEM.

(F) *Foster care Services for the victims, who have not been accepted by their parents,* should be promoted to facilitate their social rehabilitation. Arrangements for marriage or rehabilitation must be done only after proper verification of the groom by the Protective Homes.

(G) *Suitable amendments to the Acts like the Children Act have to be made to legalise the process of dissociation of a child from its mother on the understanding* that the child's future development would become the state's responsibility and would not result in breaking the family tie.

(H) *Involvement of selected individuals and voluntary organisations:* The necessity of involving selected individuals and voluntary organisations as collaborating partners in government efforts is vital.

Such individuals and voluntary agencies could supplement and complement governmental efforts by securing the involvement of the families from which the girls come. Such voluntary agencies could be the motivators among such backward families and help in bringing about change of their attitude and also of the other members of the society. They can also assist in—

(i) Awareness building about the causes and consequences of flesh trade, and traditional practices supporting it,

(ii) Involvement and mobilisation of the people in the prevention and control of the problems,

(iii) Counselling and guiding victims of the trade,

(iv) Initiating development programme and low cost and experimental rehabilitation programmes, including foster care and child care services,

(v) Assisting in rescue operations in redlight areas,

(vi) Working as a watchdog and the eyes and ears of the people in ensuring that women are not exploited as sex objects,

(vii) Providing legal aid to the victims,

(viii) Organising or collaborating in the organisation of training programmes for persons involved in the prevention and control of the trade.

(I) *To enable the selected voluntary organisations and individuals to perform,* Government must provide the necessary financial and technical assistance, besides organisational support, and security.

Mass awareness, building for attitudinal development, with comprehensive development and rehabilitation programmes and intensification of administrative and legal action along with involvement of selected people and voluntary organisations could prove very constructive in reducing the evil effects of the flesh trade and thereby trafficking.

LACK OF SYSTEMATIC WORK

What is required is systematic police action in a big way not normally to resume a fair victims by occasional raids on brothels but also the investigate thoroughly the modus operandi of the recketeers their area of practice their contacts at various levels and the pattern of their operations in all ramifications.

ANTI-OBSCENITY

The police are annoyed. The few policemen who bother enough about the outpouring of pornographic magazines, films and video tapes, find they cannot use a bill specially enacted to punish the indecent portrayal of women and the bring the offenders to book because the Government has time to publish it in the official gazette and formalise it into law. Today pornographic material—books, videos and films is being sold at prices which would have appeared impossibly high just two years ago. At a time when people are groaning under rising prices, thousands are paying exorbitant sums for pornoraphic material, which is now bought faster then it is produced. Wretchedly designed magazines, nothing more than hastily produced photostat collections, of pornographic photographs, are selling at Rs. 100 a copy. Video tapes which are smudged pirated versions of their American originals can be hired at triple the cost of an ordinary tape—that is after you have paid a Rs. 300 deposit for borrowing them.

If the market for such material is to be believed, it is the 'hard porn' which fetches the highest prices. And by this is meant not just photographs or descriptions of nudity, or the supposedly subtle ways in which women are seen as objects to be enjoyed as much as our favorite brand of the cigarette or liquor. All this is vastly interesting. But it is material describing in explicit details the sexual subjugation of women that fetches the highest returns. The inherent violence in such deceptions, the extent to which they degrade women and present them in utter subjugation to men is that these "gourmet readers" rush out to buy any specimen at any price.

How do you deal with all this? Tolerating its existence is no answer, particularly when it is women who pay dearly of such material. While there are no Indian studies on the direct correlation between violence against women and pornography, there are enough data to confirm suspicions that pornography can spur people with a disregard for the law into act of violence like rape, particularly when they are fed on the notions that women may actually enjoy such violence. So when women's organizations protest against pornography, they are not clamouring for a return to Victorian when women's form was own as evil, as rousing "baser passions" or "corrupting" men. No, women are protesting against the inherent violence that pornography condones.

MAIN DEMAND

It is to their credit that such concerned people have had the foresight not to advocate sweeping laws which infringe on a person's right to free expression. Nor are they saying the police should have the power to act arbitrarily against all those considered purveyors of pornographic material or take upon themselves the task of guarding "public morality" and ad hoc definitions of what is obscene: It was after much debate and analysts that concerned women's and civil rights organisations across the country agreed that the present laws dealing with obscenity were inadequate.

Section 292 of the Indian Penal Code deals with the issue in a way which is broad enough to permit free speech (a constitutional right yet nonetheless subject to "reasonable restrictions") and erotica without excessively abridging either. The section bans any publication which is 'lascivious' which 'appeals to prurient interests' or "deprave" or "corrupts" the viewer. There are two fundamental problems with this law. First, it does not provide a near-accurate working description of obscenity—which begs the question of whether it is at all description of obscenity—which begs the question of whether it is all possible to lay down water-tight definitions about this issue in the first place. Next, it did not deal with the hundreds of posters, advertisements, photographs which feed the notion that women exist for male pleasure.

One outcome of such concern was the 1986 Indecent Representation of Women (Prohibition) Bill. It neatly side-stepped these issues by simply prohibiting the "indecent representation of women through advertisements or the publications, writings, paintings, figures or in any other manner." The Bill has given the police the authority to enter and search "at all reasonable times" any place in which the police have reason to believe that such an offence is committed. The police cannot enter any private dwelling without a warrant. The fines are also much higher—those caught on the first offence shall be punishable with imprisonment for two years or a fine extending to Rs. 2,000. Subsequent offence shall be punishable with fines of not less than Rs. 10,000 but extending upto one lakh of rupees and imprisonment of not less than six months and extending upto five years. Too harsh, gentle readers? Nay if you consider the enormous profits, most of them unaccounted ones, which purveyors of this material shall reap through their sales.

What happens today after a police official raids a book-stall or a library which sells such material under Section 292 of the IPC? The offence of obscenity is cognisable which means the police have the power to arrest without a warrant. But the offence is bailable. In other words, spend a week quietly investigating into the details of such an establishment—where it gets its supply of obscene material, who are the people connected with its production and sales, what are the sources and once you nab the culprits, what do they do? Go find a lawyer who bails them out within hour. Stop for a moment and think of the contempt with which, otherwise such honest officers (and the breed dose exist) look at such a law. Several months later when the case comes up before the court, how does the magistrate deal with the issue? Sometimes he titters, other times he looks bored, slams a fine of Rs. 200 and turns to the next case.

The Assistant Commissioner of Police who heads Bombay city's vigilance branch, Mr. Minto Irani, spoke with anger and pride about his efforts to "clean up" the city, insists the 1986 Bill would make his work both more effective and enduring. What he and his vigilance squad have picked of the street is sheer filth, the sales of which cannot be justified on any ground. While those selling or producing such material can be caught under the IPC, the stringent punishments described in the 1986 Bill cannot be applied to them. How does a fine of Rs. 2,000 paid after two years, deter those flogging such sales? Next, the IPC does not permit the police to enter such places without a warrant, which is usually prepared after the police have cleared the matter with their legal experts and concluded it as obscenity. With all the precautions against unjust or arbitrary police action—except that by the time the police swings into action, the material is out on the streets and into eager hands.

COURT VS CENSORS

While inaugurating the platinum jubilee celebrations of Indian Cinema in Madras on April 18, 1989 the President

Mr. R. Venkataraman said: " Entertainment must not be at the expense of values: box office successes ought not to be won by pandering to baser instincts. No pair of scissors, howsoever honestly and diligently applied, can be more effective than industry's own pair of scissors." The President's remarks, which obliquely commented on the system of film censorship that has prevailed since the enactment of the Cinematograph Act, come at an opportune moment when attention is focussed on the issue because of the Supreme Court decision in the case of a film banned by the Central Board of Film Certification (CBFC).

The film, in question, may not be the worst example of what the studios of Hollywood can produce. But it just happens to be one that contravened a censorship guideline, which was recently introduced to curb the trend towards images on the silver screen that were seen to denigrate women.

AGAINST GUIDELINE

The guideline stipulates that visuals or words depicting women in ignoble servility to man or glorifying such servility as a praiseworthy quality should not be presented. Both the examining committee of the CBFC consisting of five members and the revising committee consisting of five members and the revising committee consisting of seven members recommended that the film be refused a certificate. The producer of the film then went to the film certification appellate tribunal which has three members. The tribunal was of the firm view that the film could not be passed as it contravened a number of guidelines. "No amount of cuts will, in our opinion, change or tone down the objectionable impact of the film. We have, therefore, no hesitation in upholding the decision of the Board."

It was after this that the court came into the picture. In his writ petition before the Bombay High Court, the producer appealed not just against the particular decision of the Board and the Tribunal but also questioned the guidelines under which the ban was justified stating that as the constitution had special provisions for women, they did not need such guidelines to protect them. The film in question, "Pati Parmeshwar, presents a particularly difficult problem because the theme is so inextricably linked with the popular concept of "tradition". It depicts the "good" wife being prepared to do anything, even to pretend to be a servant while her husband openly pursues another woman. In the end, however, her patience and commitment to the institution of marriage pays of, her husband repents and comes back to her.

EXEMPLIFYING VIRTUES

In his judgement on the film, Bombay High Court Judge, Justice S.C. Pratap, while station that the ban on the film was not sustainable, held that the heroine of the film, the wife "exemplified the inner strength and character of Indian womanhood." In his view "her commitment to marriage is total and supreme and she honours it in full measure in the true spirit of Hindu ethyls". She could have walked out of the marital home. "It was so every easy. But no. Nothing doing. She boldly rejects, that self-centered path, it was contrary to her father's advice and blessings, in consonance with the very substratum of Hindu view of life and marriage, it was also contrary to the hallowed traditions of Hindu society; and it was destructive of the sanctity and piousness inherent in the sacred institution of marriage. A true *soubhagyavati,* she steadfastly holds on to the higher values which, in many a matrimonial home today, are seen falling by the wayside." He asks whether a film based on such a theme could be banned and answers that he thinks not.

On the other hand, in justifying its decision to ban the film, the tribunal had held that the film "tries to promote ideas not in keeping with the values of present-day society".

Unfortunately, this is where its decisions can be faulted; because it can be argued that in fact the film reflects present day values, however, undesirable they might be. In fact, every new incident of dowry death, such as the recent horrifying incident of 21-year-old Shalini Malhotra in New Delhi's Defence Colony being set on fire with whisky by a drunken husband, illustrates only too starkly what are present day values, where a true *soubhagyavati* is expected to hold on to her marriage, regardless. Yet, this is precisely the reason why some people feel such films should be banned. They argue that it is not just films that blatantly justify violence against women which harm women's status in society but also those that reinforce all those beliefs and traditions which justify women's inferior status in the family and in society. In that respect, themes such as the one in "Pati Parmeshwar", which glorify servility in the name of tradition are extremely regressive.

The "Pati Parmeshwar" matter should not be viewed as a stray case for it could be indicative of a new trend in the mass media which reflects the increasing emphasis on tradition that is now a popular theme in politics. At the same time, whether the system of film censorship can curb such a trend or not is debatable. The CBFC, specially under the Chairmanship of Mr. Bikram Singh, who was recently forced to step down, did make a serious attempt to implement the censorship guidelines as also to generate discussion on the difficulties and the desirability of censorship. It is highly unlikely, however, that the present CBFC will stick so diligently either to the letter or the spirit of the censorship guidelines in the future following the Supreme Court's decision upholding the Bombay High Court judgement in the *"Pati Parmeshwar"* case.

HIGH-PROFILE MEET

Last year, a high-profile conference was held in Bombay on the question of film censorship. Members from different boards were present to meet representatives of the film industry, film critics, ministers, bureaucrats from the concerned ministries and jounalists. At this meeting, the film industry representatives made a strong plea for self-regulation. They argued that the system of film censorship created distortions and their films would be much better if they were not treated as errant schoolboys to be disciplined and watched over.

It is plain, however, that the only kind of regulation that the commercial cinema understands is that of the market. Today, film-makers have to contend not only with video but also with the wide reach of television. Increasingly, the role that the "family drama" type of film used to play is being fulfilled by television serials. It is hardly surprising, therefore, that this genre of film has disappeared almost completely.

The video boom has drastically affected both the type of audience for popular cinema and the numerous video-films. In the cities, particularly, cinema halls are almost wholly dominated by youth, a majority of them male, unemployed or under employed. Films cater to this audience and whether there is a system of censorship or self-regulation, film makers will seek ways to hold no to his audience by providing the kind of violent and coarse fare that has become the by-word in commercial cinema.

A study of the impact of censorship on the quality of films, especially with regard to the portrayal of women, is needed before we can determine whether it has been effective or not. Such a study would be relevant at this stage when, amongst other things, recommendations under the national perspective plan for women on the question of women and the media are being debated and finalised.

3

SEX IN TOURISM INDUSTRY

INTRODUCTION

The tourism industry cannot be held accountable for the behaviour of its clients, unless the industry involves them in (commercial) sex opportunities. But it is always affirmed by those who promote tourism that the fundamental objective for the industry is "to promote peace, human rights, mutual understanding, respect for all peoples and cultures and sustainable development". It is encouraging to see that a number of tourism bodies are taking these objectives seriously and there is a new sense of corporate responsibility among many branches of the tourism industry. This is seen particularly in the growing awareness of the need to protect the environment from the impact of too much tourism on some fragile eco-systems. Tourism must respect the environment and people. In terms of tourism.s promotion of human rights, respect for all people and sustainable development, there is clearly an issue to be resolved in the general area of .sex tourism. This blanket phrase, "sex tourism", first used by non-governmental organisations in 1980 to describe the phenomenon in South-East Asia, is now seen by many countries as contrary to sustainable economic and human development. Several tourism organisations have established trade conventions which ensure that tour agencies which promote sex-tours will forfeit their licence to remain as tour agents. This is sometimes done in response to public pressure. During the Swiss ECPAT campaign in 1992, a journalist arranged a child sex-tour through a travel agent and on his return home he wrote an exposition of the agent.s operation. The subsequent public outcry ensured that the agent was no longer able to operate his business.

In introducing laws of extraterritoriality to end child prostitution, several countries, including the United States, Germany and Australia, have also incorporated legal provisions which prohibit the operation of child-sex tours. Any tour operator who attempts to promote child-sex tours now faces the possibility of fine or imprisonment. Sex tourism has thus created a "web-work" in which tourists, the sex industry and the tourism industry itself are involved either by necessity or by implication, by intention or not.

Tourists seek factual information on the place to be visited. Beyond their primary need for prices, timetables etc., they are also given background information on social and cultural customs and restrictions in the country they are visiting. Therefore, as a first level of action, education about child sexual abuse needs to be a major priority. In the last three years numerous groups have initiated some actions in this regard. Often it has been done as a partnership between the tourism industry and governments or the tourism industry and non-governmental organisations. Some examples:

TRAVEL AGENTS

Since 1993 a number of countries have passed laws of extraterritoriality which means that nationals from that country who sexually abuse children overseas can be tried for the crime in their home country. To inform the public of this new law several countries have produced material for the use of travellers.

Sweden

The Swedish aid agency Rädda Barnen helped produce an imaginative card to be inserted in airline tickets to Asia. One side gave .the bright side. of tourism and the other .the dark side.. The latter warned tourists that they should protect children--not exploit them. Cards were distributed by the Swedish Travel Agency Association.

Norway

Redd Barna and Den Norske Reisebransjeforeningen co-operated to produce a widely-distributed brochure warning against AIDS and child prostitution.

France

The French travel industry and several government ministries have combined to produce a leaflet which warns against child prostitution. Distributed through travel agents, more than 300,000 copies were distributed in the first months and by now over 1 million have been given out.

CUSTOMS

Australia

The Australian customs service has a supply of leaflets at the counter. They are available to anyone, but one is often directly handed to male travellers going to one of the Asian sex-tourism destinations. The leaflet warns against child sex tourism. It was initiated by ECPAT-Australia and funded by aid agencies. New Zealand is preparing a similar brochure.

IN FLIGHT

Germany

During long flights travellers are receptive to some low-key information on the issue. Already in the late seventies and early eighties, Condor flights to Colombo/Sri Lanka successfully showed a 28 minute film on how tourists should not behave. Responses to begging children, behaviour and dressing in sacred sites and temples as well as the personal and social relationship of tourists with a 12-year-old beach boy were topics treated in the film with sensitivity.

Indonesia

Garuda airlines became concerned at the activities of tourists to Indonesia in the 1980s and inserted a brochure in the seat pocket of all their flights from Australia and America to Indonesia. This contained a Code of Ethics for travellers.

Italy

The Italian Federation of Travel and Tourism has declared its willingness to distribute a leaflet and this will probably be done in association with Alitalia airlines.

Austria

A negative example from Lauda Air, the Austrian airline shows that the issue of child sex abuse is not something which can be treated lightly. In 1992 the inflight magazine of Lauda Air contained an offensive mock postcard from a German tourist. The photo was a young Thai girl naked from the waist up and the message on the back boasted of the pleasures of sex in a bar in Thailand. "Must go", the message ended, "the tarts in the Baby Club are waiting for me". It was a particularly tasteless and insensitive piece of journalism and led to public protests in Bangkok and eventually a qualified apology from Lauda Air.

ON THE GROUND

Thailand

Groups concerned at the sexual abuse of children produced a pamphlet in 1995 to be widely distributed to foreign tourists through hotels and some shops. Produced by the National Commission on Women.s Affairs, it carries the message "Sex with Children is a Crime".

THROUGH GUIDE BOOKS

United States

Fodors guide books and videos are the authoritative American guide to travel. Fodors has taken an interest in the campaign against child prostitution and featured it on television programmes. They also include a Code of Ethics in many of their books.

Australia

Lonely Planet is one of the largest travel publications in the world and the company has recently set up a watching brief on issues such as political repression, indigenous rights, ecological damage, the environmental impact of tourism and now child prostitution. In relation to child sex tourism, Lonely Planet believes it has a responsibility to help raise awareness of the sexual exploitation of children, especially in countries where this is particularly acute. To this end it has been sending ECPAT-Australia.s information kits to authors contracted to update Lonely Planet editions. The aim is to ensure that their authors are informed and address the issue of child sex tourism as well as the recent changes to national and international law which make this activity a criminal offence.

AT TRAVEL FAIRS

United Kingdom

In several countries national travel exhibitions have had displays warning against child sex tourism prepared by local non-governmental organisations. The United Kingdom is one of several examples. In the UK the Coalition on Child Prostitution and Tourism was given a free stand by the Association of British Travel Agents for a display at the 1995 World Travel Mart.

COOPERATION: EMPLOYERS/EMPLOYEES

Joint efforts by employers and employees in tourism facilities such as hotels and hostels can assist to ensure that the sexual exploitation of children is prevented or, if it occurs, is reported and cases are put into the hand of law-enforcement officials. Already, the IUF/UITA/IUL (International Union of Food, Agricultural, Hotel, Restaurant, Catering, Tobacco and Allied Workers. Association) has passed resolutions to this effect in June 95 and December 95 stating that workers in the tourism sector can and must play a key-role in the fight against child prostitution. and calling for negotiations with employers for appropriate joint action. The IUF/ UITA/IUL also .underscores the key responsibility of governments in this struggle, both in host countries and in the home countries of tourists., and .urges governments to intensify their efforts aimed at enforcing human rights, in particular for children, by enacting appropriate legislation that makes it a crime for individuals or businesses to promote or engage in business involving child prostitution..

In Which Countries is This Abuse of the Young Most Common? The United Nations Children's Fund (UNICEF) said the illegal nature of child sex tourism and the involvement of organised crime makes it difficult to obtain reliable data. In Thailand, for example, estimates of the number of child prostitutes vary from 15,000 by the Ministry of Public Health to 30,000 by the Thai Red Cross to 200,000 by ECPAT. The latter figure includes girls brought to Thailand from countries such as Myanmar and Vietnam.

According to UNICEF, studies by Thammasat University in Bangkok claimed the sex industry in Thailand generates US $1.5 billion a year.

Indonesia's ministry of social affairs said 60 per cent of 71,281 registered prostitutes are aged 15-20.

How Serious a Problem is Child Sex Tourism in Asia? According to the international campaign group, End Child Prostitution in Asian Tourism (ECPAT), one million children in Asia are involved in prostitution. These include 300,000 in India, 200,000 in Thailand, 100,000 in the Philippines and 40,000 in Vietnam. And, said Ms. Christine Beddoe, ECPAT's information officer in Bangkok, numbers are increasing.

She said: "New countries such as Cambodia and Laos have documented increases in child prostitution as well as countries that have had a longer history such as Thailand and the Philippines."

Religion has played a role.

"Some rites and traditions which are present in the Buddhist and Hindu religions are abused to sexually exploit children for commercial purposes," said Mr. Henryk Handszuh, chief of the World Tourism Organisation's (WTO) quality of tourism development section.

What is being Done by Governments in Asia to Control the Problem? Governments in Asia have not turned a blind eye. "New legislation in some countries—Thailand, the Philippines, Sri Lanka, Cambodia—(has resulted in) harsher penalties for sex offenders and pimps or brothel owners," said Ms. Beddoe.

In addition, Thailand has expressed interest in joining WTO's Tourism and Child Prostitution Watch, a task force of public and private sector groups formed to encourage self-regulation within the tourism industry. Japan is considering a law to allow child sex offenders to be prosecuted in their home countries for crimes committed elsewhere.

But the Indian Government has a different approach.

"There has never been a problem as far as child sex tourism goes in India," said Mr. Ashok Pahwa, Director-General of the Department of Tourism. "There is no question of taking action when the problem does not exist."

Where are the Source Markets for Paedophiles?

ECPAT statistics reveal the majority of- but not all—arrested abusers come from the West and Australia.

"This is not just a 'western' problem," said Ms. Beddoe. "Many child sex tourists come from Asia as well, (including) all major travel outbound markets."

In Vietnam, for example, children's charity, Swedish Save Children, told TTG Asia that source countries are Asian, mainly from Taiwan and Hong Kong, who prefer children aged 14-15. Sex tours from Japan to the Philippines, Taiwan and Thailand are increasing and, according to ECPAT, a case in Thailand against a Japanese man is still pending. In India, where 5,000 girls are forced into prostitution each year, local males are the culprits. ECPAT said Taiwan faces a similar situation, as 40,000-60,000 children are "visited" by Taiwanese men and Asian business travellers.

If Many of the Paedophiles are from Europe and the US, Surely the Issue is Out of the Control of Asian Travel Companies?

Airlines, hotels and tour operators are usually the tourists' first contact in their destination, and thus have some control. "From our experience, we know that the staff often pick up on the first clues," said Ms. Beddoe.

This can work both ways. To promote child sex tourism, Ms. Yujolwadee of the Centre for the Protection of Children

Rights in Bangkok, said: "(Tour) guides in Thailand usually suggest places to have sex with children". Mr. Handszuh said: "Asian travel companies cannot directly control child sex exploiters for their behaviour, but they can help by adopting a common anti-sex tourism awareness and attitude."

Isn't This a Moral Question Beyond the Scope of Travel Agents and Tour Operators?

Both ECPAT and the WTO believe travel agents and tour operators are morally responsible, even if they are only indirectly involved.

"The travel industry is not responsible for child sex tourism but it does provide a vehicle for easy access to vulnerable children," said Ms. Beddoe.

So What can the Travel Trade do to Help Stop the Spread of this Menace?

Ms. Beddoe suggested: "First, by being informed—training of staff must be a priority and a responsibility of training schools, management and the media.

"Second, by using brochures, in-flight information, window stickers and so forth to declare (the company's) condemnation of child sex tourism.

"Third, by not being complacent.

"Fourth, by passing on information to the authorities—especially information concerning fellow members of the trade. Do not turn a blind eye."

Mr. Handszuh said: "Travel operators may commercially sanction (for example, cancel contracts) with hotels and resorts which facilitate or allow child prostitution on their premises. This is a solution used by the 12 largest German tour operators."

Where can Agents and Operators Obtain More Information and How can They Join the Campaign?"

"The logical way for agents and operators in Asia would be to co-operate with ECPAT which knows the problems in the field, and has support from tourist origin countries for Asia," said Mr. Handszuh.

Ms. Beddoe welcomed the suggestion. "Just give us the address details and we will add them to our mail-list for newsletters and updates."

Are There Examples of Effective Trade Action to Combat Sex Tourism?

While some have adopted preventive measures, ECPAT and the WTO believe more should be done to involve every individual, frontliners and management alike. The measures already instituted in some Asian countries were initiated by the trade itself.

According to ECPAT, hotel associations in Kaoshiung and Taipei initiated campaigns among members, who are asked to display anti-child prostitution cards at the hotel reception and to give discounts to ECPAT supporters. Indonesian flag carrier, Garuda Airlines, took action in the 1980s, with brochures in the seat pockets of all flights from Australia and the US to Indonesia. The brochures contain a code of ethics for travellers.

Some Thai hotels and shops in Thailand have been distributing pamphlets since 1995 to foreign tourists. Carrying the message "sex with children is a crime", the leaflets were produced by the National Commission on Women's Affairs.

A lack of knowledge among tour operators has also led to a complacent attitude. Some agents in India acknowledge the fact that backpacking paedophiles from the west have been attracted to Goa's northern beaches, but felt this was not a problem and it would not spread to the rest of the country.

Mr. Handszuh said child prostitution in Asia becomes more acute with poverty. The situation is aggravated by the lack of foreign aid, essential if the travel trade in these countries is to successfully eradicate the problem.

Mr. Roger Walker, charity World Vision Australia's senior policy adviser, said: "This year's (Australian) budget promised the world's poor the lowest level of assistance in 25 years."

SELF REGULATION

From within the tourism industry there have been several creative proposals for monitoring what is happening and for self-regulation. Two of the more interesting developments in this regard come from Taiwan and Germany:

Taiwan

Following an NGO report of 1993, which revealed a very high number of child prostitutes in Taiwan, the Kaoshiung Hotel Association and the Taipei Hotel Association initiated campaigns among their members to support ECPAT in combating child prostitution in Asian tourism. They discipline any of their members known to encourage child prostitution in their rooms. Other actions include:

- hanging anti-child-prostitution plastic cards in front of the hotel reception,
- issue of VIP cards for ECPAT supporters, entitling the holder to discounts in the participating hotels (50,000 cards issued so far),

- a statement by the Kaoshiung Hotel Association in support of ECPAT, expressing commitment to help victims of child prostitution and mentioning the actions taken.

Germany

On the basis of a draft, Terre Des Hommes Germany made contracts with 12 German tour operators to date, in which the signatories undertake to:

- ensure that there will be no child prostitution in their partner hotels,
- inform their customers about the background and impact of child prostitution,
- train their staff in hotel and tour guides accordingly.

CHILD SEX TOURISM IN COMBODIA

There is growing interest in Combodia as a vacation destination, but Combodia also is a destination for thousands of men from around the world seeking sex with children. As other developing countries such as Thailand make progress in reducing sex tourism, opportunistic men simply travel to poorer, less developed neighbouring countries.

As one of the world's 20 poorest countries, Combodia is ripe for such exploitation. Its 11.4 million people have an average income of only $ 300 annually. Its social, political and legal institutions still are recovering from the brutal legacy of the Khmer Rouge. Access to health care and education is very limited. Young girls are especially prone to drop out of school to help support their families.

At the same time, tourism is on the rise. Most visitors come to Combodia for the rich heritage and natural beauty exemplified by Angkor Wat. The Combodian government, which considers tourism to be a valuable part of its economic future, expects the number of foreign visitors to triple over the next three years.

Unfortunately, sex tourism also is on the rise in Combodia. One-third of all sex workers in the country are estimated to be children, mostly ages 12 to 17, but some even younger.

In a recent survey in conjunction with Combodia's tourism ministry and its National Council for Children, World Vision found that 45 per cent of Combodian travel agents said they had seen tour guides supply children to foreign visitors. More than 70% of children surveyed around Angkor Wat and nearby towns said that tourists had approached them for sex.

REPORTING THE CRIME

The sexual abuse or trafficking of a child is a crime and must be reported. However, many people prefer to look the other way when they suspect that there is some abuse taking place, while others are reluctant to report for fear of losing their jobs. Reporting is the task of everyone in the field: the tourism industry (tourism companies, trade organizations) individuals employed by the tourism industry (tourism personnel) and the travelling public. In addition, NGOs and private citizens in a given destination could and should report relevant facts and observations. Last, but by no means least, all media have to play a vital role to ensure that facts are brought into the open. Appropriate legislation by governments and self-regulation measures by all sectors of the tourism industry provide a useful and necessary framework for personal action and will encourage any voluntary action based on conscience, sensibility and awareness. The following cases illustrate that some courageous and active responses to this challenge do take place:

India

In 1991 a hostess on Indian Airlines noticed a young girl in distress. Speaking to her in her own dialect she discovered that she was a young girl sold by her parents and being abducted to Saudi Arabia by the man next to her. The hostess radioed to the police in Delhi, announced to the passengers what was happening and got them to sign a petition. The abductor was arrested and the girl freed.

Thailand

In 1993 a French group tour included some single men. When one of the men told his friend that he was going to have sex with a child the friend was outraged. There was a loud argument but the first man finally decided to go and have sex with a young child anyway. The second man went to the police and made them arrest his countryman. It may seem an attractive proposal to encourage those in the tourism industry to report a crime or the potential for a crime but the idea must be approached with caution. The semblance of criminality does not necessarily mean that a crime is about to occur. The proposal also gives the possibility of persons fulfilling a vendetta against their enemies.

LOBBYING GOVERNMENTS

In recent years laws to cover the commercial sexual abuse of children in tourism have been passed in Germany (June 1993), France (February 1994), Australia (July 1994), United States (September 1994), Belgium (March 1995) and New Zealand (July 1995) with several other countries considering similar measures. In most cases the government has received submissions from the tourism industry and from tourism ministries. The submissions were in all cases positive in their support of legislation. In Italy the government passed an Order of the Day (March 1995) which requires travel agents to comply with the Convention on the Rights of the Child, particularly the commercial sexual exploitation of children.

TRAINING PROGRAMMES

Lufthansa and Air New Zealand are among the airlines which have included instruction of their staff on the dangers of commercial child sex exploitation in their regular training programmes. A number of other airlines are discussing the possibility.

CONCLUSION

The Congress will provide an opportunity for Governments to review their own role in the determination of tourism policies. In many instances political action will be essential to ensure that child sex tourism is prevented. A cooperative partnership between governments and tourism could make a positive contribution to ending the commercial sexual exploitation of children.

4

COMMERCIAL SEX AND LAW

The change in public perception and consequent variations in legislative policies have been influenced by public and health conditions, law and order concerns, attitudes towards sex and morality, human rights standards and most importantly in the light of the UN Conferences of the past decade, the issue of women's status and gender justice. The problem involved in the immoral trafficking of persons, generally associated with commercial sex work is differently perceived at varying tines both by the people and by the government. In the process of changes in public perceptions and attitudes, the enforcement of legislative policy suffered a great tended to prevent commercial exploitation of sex, what actually resulted is corruption in the enforcement machinery and wider exploitation in more surreptitious ways often with the protection of the so-called law enforcement apparatus. The challenge for those NGOs and Social Workers concerned with the issue of commercial sex work is more in the manner of the enforcement of the law than the sex industry itself. Though the manifestations of the sex industry are posing serious threats to human dignity, public health and morality and to women's rights. This is the agenda that legislative reform must aim to address.

Four decades ago, in the Convention of 1949, when the United Nation called for decriminalization of the transaction called "prostitution" India respondent—as most countries—with the Suppression of Immoral Traffic in Women and Girls Act 1956.

The Act which only retained criminality in respect of living off the earnings of a "prostitute", serving as a ho-between running a flesh trade business, publicity soliciting, and "transporting women" across national borders for neither abolish nor legalize commercial sex work. Those who promote penalties against customers and agents whether or not coercion was involved tend to equate "prostitution" with rope and "prostitutes" clearly as victims of these transaction. This viewpoint therefore makes it impossible to create a context in which working conditions could be legally improved.

On the other hand, those calling for "legalization" generally want to license or register the women concerned and thus require them to have regular health checks and stop working when they are unable to do so medically—due to AIDS or other such related diseases. This line of thinking also advocates licensed brothels and consequently leaving women not legalized outside the licensed premises. This approach endorses State Control with no concern for the women involved in the profession.

Viewing these two approaches objectively has furthered yet another line of approach of decriminalization. Acknowledging sex work or sexual services as labour this theory argues that sex workers should have legitimate right to organize and agitate safe conditions of work. It also admits the inevitability of the sex industry and condemns the abolitionist or regulationist approaches. What it therefore advocates is total decriminalization of all aspects of voluntary sex work between consenting adults. In addition it also necessitates de-criminalisation of mutually voluntary relationships between the sex workers and their agents and managers. The option opened here is to leave sex work business subject to the some laws which govern other businesses be it on safety, health or dispute settlements. Alternatively existing sections of the Penal Code could be modified to specifically address the issues of coerced sex work, and business and labour laws could be enacted to specifically extend the coverage of these laws as found necessary sex work business.

CRITICAL REVIEW—IMMORAL TRAFFIC IN PERSONS PREVENTION ACT 1986

An increasingly large number of young girls and women are driven to the flesh trade every year. Finding an expending market, more and more victims are lured from the countryside and even from neighboring countries of Nepal and Bangladesh. The Indian Constitution prohibits immoral trafficking in view of its various forms and shades of violating human rights and dignity, especially of women.

The problem of trafficking is complex and places the State under obligation to the Constitution and International Instrument to find satisfactory solution to address this challenge. Whilst not denying the right of voluntary sexual relations of any citizen, the commercialization of this profession is detrimental to women and girls as also to the social and public health of all persons. In pursuance of the International Convention of 1949 the Suppression of Immoral Traffic in Women and Girls Act 1956 was enacted. This Act was amended in 1978 and again in 1986 to rectify some of the inadequacies in the implementation of the Act. However, these amendments have in no way addressed the complex and vest dimensions of immoral trafficking.

THE ACT

The Immoral Traffic in Persons Prevention Act 1986 (ITPPA) was passed in the winter session of Parliament 1986. This Act is an amendment to the Suppression of

Immoral Traffic in Women and Girls Act 1956 (SITA), and was passed primarily in the context of the latter's failure to suppress traffic in women and girls for commercial sex purposes. The basic aims, objectives, logic and premises of the ITPPA remain similar to the SITA. However, the ITPPA does introduce several positive amendments. At the same time the 1986 Act retains the clauses in the SITA used to penalize the women in prostitution but leaves much to be desired in its provisions for rehabilitation and general implementation.

PENALTIES FOR FACILITATING COMMERCIALIZED SEX-WORK

The Immoral Traffic (Prevention) Act lays down penalties for keeping a brothel or allowing premises to be used as a brothel; living on earnings of prostitution; procuring, inducing and inducting persons for the sake of prostitution; detaining a person in premises where prostitution is carried on; prostitution in or in the vicinity of public place and soliciting for purpose of prostitution.

Therefore those who abet in making people go for prostitution, those who detain persons in premises where prostitution is carried on and those who allow premises or vehicles to be used for the sake of prostitution are guilty of facilitating prostitution and are liable to be punished.

PRESUMPTIONS UNDER THE ACT

The Immoral Traffic (Prevention) Act prescribes stringent action against persons with children in a brothel. The Court may presume that a child found in a brothel or under suspicious circumstances in the custody of a person other than the parent or lawful guardian who is unable to explain satisfactorily the presence of such a child has procured the child for purposes of prostitution.

Furthermore if these children are found, on medical examination, to be sexually abused, it is presumed—by the Act-that the children have been sexually exploited for commercial purpose.

The punishment could be imprisonment life, or for a term that may extend to 10 years. The Court may further presume that a child found accompanying, in suspicious circumstances, a person who is neither its parent or lawful guardian and who is leaving the country is committing the offense of immoral trafficking.

The Act clearly states that sexual intercourse with a woman with or without her consent if she is under 16 years of age amounts to rape and hence the offenders are punishable upto imprisonment for life.

The various provisions of the Immoral Traffic (Prevention) Act (ITPA) are enforced through the local police structures, duly empowered under Section 13(1) and (3) of the Act. The lack of specialized police officers, therefore, results in the simple arrests of the women in this trade who are only the apparent manifestations of the problem, but the more insidious and criminal aspects of trafficking, coercion, violence and commercial exploitation normally do not get investigated and acted against in a sustained manner. Strong allegations have been made against the police in that they and the local mafia are being paid by the sex-workers/brothel keepers and other confers while vested interests conspire to ensure the continuance of this exploitative system.

DEFINITIONAL CHANGES

The Act introduces definitional distinctions between an adult, minor and child and changes in the definition of "prostitution". The expression of "prostitute" is to be construed as "the sexual exploitation or abuse of persons for commercial purposes" a variation from the earlier definition of "the act of a female offering her body for promiscuous sexual intercourse for hire, whether in money or kind". The new definition has been widened to include (a) both male and female prostitution and (b) any form of sexual exploitation or abuse for commercial purposes, instead of narrowly restricting prostitution to "promiscuous sexual intercourse."

BROTHEL—The definition of a brothel is likewise widened to include any place used for the purpose of sexual exploitation or abuse. This broader definition of a brothel would make it easier to prosecute brothel keepers under section 3 of the Act for all kinds of sexual abuse and exploitation which any not strictly amount to sexual intercourse alone.

PROTECTIVE HOME—Under the SITA a protective home refers to an institution where women and girls rescued from "prostitution" are kept in protective custody. The ITPPA incorporates and additional clause stating that such a home must have appropriate technically qualified persons, equipment and facilities. Protective homes are mandated to receive, besides those sent by a Court or Welfare Board, "all women who either on their own submission or on written statement of an NGO working for the welfare of women, seek admission to a protective home on grounds of moral danger". The State Government will make special rules for these women and the home will be regulated accordingly.

The distinction made by SITA between a woman and girl, defines the former as one who is 21 years of age or older an the latter as below 21 years of age. This distinction is made in view of the nature of rehabilitation to be provided for a woman and a girl and is based on the assumption that a woman has the right decide whether or not she should stay in prostitution, while a girl cannot. Consequently, while a woman is tried in Court, if she is booked for prostituting in a public place or soliciting, and then convicted, acquitted or referred to a protective home or corrective institution, a girl rescued from a brothel is immediately referred for rehabilitation to a protective home or corrective institution.

The inclusion of the definition of a child in the new Act, is firstly a recognition of the existence of child prostitution and traffic in children for flesh trade. The importance of these distinctions, however lies in the penal measures under the Act, to be meted out to those using persons for this profession. The younger the person who is sexually exploited and abused for commercial purposes, the more stringent is the punishment for the exploiters. In contrast to the SITA, the ITPPA takes a more serious view of child prostitution.

LANDLORDS AND OWNERS—The ITPPA seeks to plug the loophold created by the SITA for landlords and owners. Under the SITA the landlords/owners avert prosecution under the cover of "lack of knowledge". But the ITPPA states that it will be presumed, until the contrary is proved, that a landlords knowingly allows or has knowledge that his premises are being used as a brothel under two circulating in his residential area states that his premises were found to be used for prostitution, as a result of a search made, and secondly if a copy of the panchanama made during the search is handed over to the landlord, thus the onus of proof is placed on the landlord conditionally.

However, this is facial because raids are seldom conducted far less reported. And in addition the landlord is hand in glove with the brothel manager (i.e. if he is not managing the brothel himself). Providing a conditionality for onus of proof is a sure loophole that landlords will use to circumvent prosecution. What is actually needed is that once a brothel is raided, it should be presumed that the landlord, unless proved to the contrary, knowingly let his premises for prostitution or knew it was being used for prostitution. The burden of proof must thus be placed on him at any cost.

The ITPPA has introduced more stringent penal measures for several categories of offenses, with the intention that such stringency will act as a deterrent to the offender. Under the SITA offenses like procuring or detaining a person for prostitution or seduction of a person in custody, on average, incurred a rigorous imprisonment on first convection for a term of between one or two years plus a fine of up to Rs. 2000/- A second conviction brought with it, on average, an imprisonment lasting between two and four years, together with a maximum fine of up to Rs. 2000.

The same offenses under the ITPPA are penalized, on average, with a minimum of seven years imprisonment which could extend to life or for a period of 14 years together with a fine. The new Act grants discretionary powers also to the court to deduce the term of imprisonment to below the seven year minimum for offenses such a detaining a person for prostitution or seduction of a person in custody.

The increasing in penal measures under the new Act is welcome but the discretionary powers to the judge to reduce the term of imprisonment below the stipulated minimum of seven years for certain offenses defeats the deterrent effect of an increase in penalties. It must therefore be binding on courts trying offenses under the Act, to give the minimum punishment laid down, if not more.

Under the SITA, punishment for seducing or soliciting for prostitution incurs an imprisonment extending to a year as the case may be. However, the new Act penalizes such an offense by a man with imprisonment for a period of not less than seven days extend able to three months.

Both the SITA and the ITPPA do not intend penalizing prostitution *per se*. But some of the clauses referring to women in prostitution are ambiguously formulated. This ambiguity is often used against the women and thus amounts to punishing the already exploited section of society. A double standard of sexual morality is indicated here for there are no penal measures for clients. Considering the magnitude in the case of forced prostitution, the Act must explicitly state who can be booked for practice of prostitution in a public place or soliciting for prostitution in order to eliminate the discrimination between buyers and providers of sex.

The amendment of 1986 has neither changed the basic frame-work nor provided any clarity on the issue. It has neither decriminalized prostitution nor offered any safety and protection against harassment and indignity. As is the case with other amendments the main thrusts of the amendment are enhancement of punishment and creation of newer categories of offenses. The Act is given a new name after the amendment and a faint sliver of progressive thinking is reflected in the fact that it recognizes that children or even men can be sexually abused and exploited for commercial purposes. However, the regressive provision which penalizes a woman in prostitution is retained in the amendment. The following are the only two provisions that could benefit a woman in the flesh trade and that too marginally :

* Recognition of the abuse of power by the police during raids amendment prohibits male officers empowered under the Act from making a search without a warrant unless accompanied by at least two women police officers. This clause not only curtails police power but also mandates a medical examination of such persons to determine age or detection of injuries caused by sexual abuse.

* Incorporation of a New Clause Concerning Rehabilitation.

The Act mandates that protective homes should not only allow women and girls to live in dignity but also to find gainful employment.

LEGALIZATION OF COMMERCIAL SEX WORK

Australia, Netherlands and Germany have adopted policies to develop a legal regime reflecting the commercial sex worker's fights. The Global Programme on AIDS is said to be evolving certain guidelines on the basic premise "that in order for sex-workers to be able to protect themselves from HIV infection AIDS, and other sexually transmitted diseases, they must have safe working conditions, including the right to turn down abusive or uncooperative clients, and the right to refuse to engage in practices likely to transmit HIV and other STD, including any penetrative sex performed without a condom."

In 1993 a Draft Bill was proposed for public discussion so that the best possible legislative policy can be evolved on the subject promoting women's rights and preventing serious health risks to people involved. The Act could be termed "The Prohibition of Immoral Trafficking and Empowerment of Sexual Workers Bill".

The rights included in this Bill could be :

* Safe Conditions of Work and Medical Assistance
* Right to refuse services on certain grounds
* Duty to ensure safe conduct and to provide safe work place
* Compensation in case of injuries and incapacitation due to STD

* Right to a Welfare Fund for sex-workers and their children

A DEBATE

While the Indian Government continues to follow the tolerationist system of law articulated in Immoral Traffic in Persons Prevention Act 1986, which has yet to be enforced, the issue of legalizing prostitution continues to be discussed and proposed by some state governments and certain medical bodies.

Proponents of legalization claim that man's sexual drive is naturally and biologically aggressive. Such an irrepressible sexuality requires prostitution as a safety valve against rampant rape and he breakdown of the family structure. Prostitution is therefore considered a universal inevitable and necessary social evil. Nevertheless, historically there is no bases for this "truth" Prostitution has existed in all class-based partriarchal societies, true, but is still unknown in many so-called primitive societies.

In recognizing the systemic causes of prostitution, the onus of responsibility is shifted from the women in prostitution to the social system and the controllers of prostitution, so much so that, in the words of Kathleen Barry "Pimping Becomes the oldest profession not prostitution".

To perceive prostitution as an inevitable and necessary social evil, is to deny the exploitative socio-economic and ideological roots of prostitution and to perceive society and its institution as immutable. This could further imply a condemnation of prostitution and perceive men as incapable like the media and pornography reinforce these patriarchal myths.

There are some who advocate legalization of prostitution because it is supposed to protect the family structure. This position is rather reactionary for it is the standard functionalist explanation which serves to conserve a patriarchal and exploitative status quo. It shies away from attaching the sexist and exploitative basis of the institution of prostitution i.e. "Male sexuality is naturally uncontainable and must find an outlet through the purchase of sex". It also shies away from challenging the oppressive basis of the patriarchal family in contemporary society, which gives the moral and legal right to a women's body in marriage exchange for financial support; endorses dual standards of morality and safeguard the purity of race and property concerns of the ruling elite and ensure a steady legitimate supply of work force. These economic functions of the patriarchal monogamous family unit, lead to the contracting of the marriage arrangements on the basis of economic status, caste, and religion. The genuine basis for a marital computability is rejected. The proliferation of such depersonalized in society coupled with double standards of morality provide the justification for males to seek pleasure outside the institution of marriage in prostitution.

THE HEALTH GROUNDS DEBATE

In a male dominated cultural setting where a woman's nature and being are defined in terms of her sexuality her reproductive organs and functions, a woman's health problems are also so defined. In this context it is no wonder that a woman in commercial sex work whose task it is to provide sex services for a price is defined in terms of a sex commodity. Consequently, the health and other problems of the women in this profession are also linked to sexuality.

Women sex-work have been historically blamed for being the source of sexually transmitted diseases. Sex-workers were looked upon as a source of deep seated social fears and insecurities. Figuratively and also literally the sex-worker was the conduit of infection to respectable society. This perception gave power of the State to exercise some control over what was perceived as dangerous have discussed the legalization and licensing of prostitution in the interest of public health.

The legalization and licensing debate initiated by the NGOs and Governments dates back to the 19th Century when Britain introduced The Contagious Disease Acts in garrison towns and ports, and which with minor modifications were also made operational on the cantonments of British India. This was done in the form of the Cantonment Act of 1864, and attempted too regulate and control female sexuality, which was perceived as dangerous, though legislation. These Acts were constructed for the specific purpose of safeguarding the men of the army and navy for "the separation from the community of women in a condition to spread contagious diseases. "The promulgation of the Act legitimized the State's manipulation and control of the female body in that, the sex-worker and not their male clients were identified as the primary source of disease.

Public health in this context implies male health, which must be maintained for the production of capital. On one hand the government is very concerned to preserve 'public health'. At times this preservation is done forcibly such as the use of the ITPPA to test sex-workers for HIV/AIDS. This line of action that of segregating the sex-workers and targeting them as being responsible for the spread of HIV/AIDS gives a false complacency to other sectors of society who feel that the disease belongs to only particular sections of society.

On the other hand the Government shows blithe unconcern for all other health problems of women in prostitution such as tuberculosis, anemia, gynecological ailments and the like. Could the lack of concern for the women on other health problems the due to the fact that it bears little or no consequence, in the eyes of the Government, for the male population?

The assumption that women to the flesh trade are more responsible for the transmission of STDs/AIDS than other groups and that state control of sex-workers will prevent such transmission is contradicted by research findings. In India, where forced and child prostitution is rampant, the woman or child enters the trade disease-free and contracts STD/HIV+ in the course of work. Blaming women in the flesh trade profession and directing policy measures against them, while forgetting the role of the client as a carrier, is an example of the sexist bias which leads to controlling and punishing the woman who is often a victim too.

The discrimination of the sex-worker in the 19th Century through the introduction of the Contagious Diseases Acts both in Britain and in Indian ports resonates in the 20th Century through the introduction of the 1989 AIDS Prevention Bill which once again targets sex-workers rather than their clients. The Bill made provisions for the health authorities to forcibly question test and isolate and HIV infected person in a hospital or "other place ... where the authority considers it necessary to do so." The Bill also gave the Health authority the discretion to decide who was considered to be at greater risk. Social activists and concerned NGOs reacted to this discriminatory which was mandated to review the bill. This pressure and reaction from these groups brought about the withdrawal of the Bill a few years later.

Legislation to reduce and control STD/HIV is useless because a woman in prostitution can be rein fected at any time between two medical examinations. Again, the experience of countries legalizing prostitution has revealed that compulsory registration of sex-workers to facilitate health checks doesn't work because sex-workers shy away from registration than ever to blackmail and impending their social mobility.

Apart from ideological disagreements with perceiving sex-workers as the source of AIDS and consequently legalizing prostitution to control the spread, legalization appears to be unpractical. For one thing the stigma attached to HIV/AIDS persons, to commercial sex workers and to the profession itself would deter the women from registering themselves as her already been shown by countries prostitution to control the spread of AIDS.

POLICE HARASSMENT AVERTED AND OTHER DEBATES

One major debate for the legalization of prostitution is the facilitation for ionization of sex-workers against police harassment and for provision of the women and their children. Examining the profiles of the existing organizations for women and their children. Examining the profiles of the existing organizations for women in the flesh trade critically, indications of a patriarchal base emerge. Thus these organizations believe in the inevitability and necessity of the institution of prostitution and also that the women involved in this profession are the source of STDs and AIDS.

Most of these organizations—e.g. The Bharatiya Patita Udhar Sabha. The Sangh floated by the India Health Organization—Asahaya Tieskrut Nari Sangh—and the Pune Devadasi Sangatna have been formed on the initiative if external agents who are males and not women in the trade. Though formal leadership is vested in the female brothel keepers who constitute the predominant membership and are the exploitative core of the hierarchically structured sex industry, the actual controls are in the hands of the male initiators of the said organizations. Again, the brothel owners in the leadership reportedly have close links with political persons or parties and thus receives his/her trade offs in return. The press publicity glorifying the philanthropic work of the male initiators and the political connections of these individuals show the underlying political and vested interests in the formation of such groups.

Demands made by the above organizations such as creche facilities and education for children of sex-workers are in the interests of the women and children common woman. The demand for legalization and licensing of prostitution is unacceptable at an ideological level, as it sanctions the patriarchal and exploitative basis of the institution of prostitution and gives brothel keepers full freedom to induct more women and girls into the trade.

The demand to abolish forced and child prostitution is farcial as the brothel owners/controlling agents are currently guilty of forcing women and children into prostitution and will continue to do so for vested interests. Then again, while the demands made to the women in the trade ultimately it works in the interests of brothel owners and pimps who pay large bribes to prevent punishment for trafficking in women and girls for prostitution. The controlling agents live off these earnings for the most part.

The demand for formation of co-operative credit societies to protect the women from money lenders is trivia. Most of the women in prostitution take loans from the controlling agents and not the money lenders, and are in constant debt to her, repaying both the principal amount and the interest. Those women who do take loans, do so on approval and consent of the brothel owners. Also, the cooperative credit societies appear to be the brothel owners strategy of obtaining low interest loans, when needed. Loans are only given to women with repaying capacity. This includes the controlling agents and a few women who have managed to save—but not the run of the mill women who are in the trade.

Separate hostel accommodations for children of the women the trade also works to the advantage of the controlling agents who would rather not have children in the way during business hours. It also serves to ghettoise and reinforce the already existing for women in prostitution and their children only reinforce segregation and stigmatization.

What is noteworthy is the absence of demands that would adversely affect the vested interests of the controlling agents. An example of this is that there is no hint is a fair wage rate for women in this profession or a just percentage of their earnings for the women versus what is currently occuring on these issues. Similarly there is no mention of hours of work for the women of limits on the number of clients that the women must entertain nor is there a promotion of a code of ethics for the controlling agents. These factors indicate that organizations—as previously mentioned and perhaps a few others too—need to be condemned rather than promoted as they are only concerned with their own betterment in the name of the women in prostitution. However, the economic factor along with pressures from the controlling agents will determine the number of customers a sex-worker will entertain.

VIABLE ALTERNATIVES

Rather than legalize prostitution as a measure of control the following steps should be considered :

(a) epidemiological studies : studies of risk factors exposing individuals and groups to infectious agents and diseases : monitoring of health and environmental factors.

(b) preventive educational programmes and motivation to high risk behaviour groups and the general populace to adopt safer sex practices. (The careful use of condoms reduces the risk of contracting the HIV/AIDS):

(c) use available infrastructure with additional inputs streng-then research and training in family welfare planning, blood banking and safe hospital practices and lastly;

(d) enforce screening of donors and good manufacturing practices for commercial concerns manufacturing blood products and blood based diagnostic agents.

In conclusion then, we may state that to advocate legislation because the ITPP Act has accomplished its objective of suppressing immoral traffic in women and children is appealing. What is needed instead is an amendment of various sections of the Act because they are in total contradiction to the stated abject and give vast powers to the police who constantly terrorize women and extract protection money out of that. For example even if a commercial sex workers support a destitute or a disabled relative she can be thrown in jail or fined or both. This is because Section 4 of the Act reads "any persons over the age of 18 years who knowingly lives wholly or in part on the earnings of prostitution for a term which may extend to two years or with which may extend to Rs. 1,000 or with both.

Furthermore a totally unexplained discrimination has been made on the grounds of sex in Section 8 of the Act. This section makes punishable the act of soliciting for the purpose of prostitution. Therefore a women can be imprisoned for a term which may extend to one year, whereas a man can only be imprisoned for a maximum term for only 3 months for the same offense. The experience of the writers has shown that this section of the act is the most abused.

What emerges than is that though the act does not aim punish one because of commercial sex workers there are enough provisions for the law to harass a women. Section 20 (1) reads : "REMOVAL OF PROSTITUTION FROM ANY PLACE : (1) A Magistrate on receiving information that any (person) residing or frequenting any place within the local limits of his jurisdiction is a prostitution may record substance of the information received and issue a notice to such (person) requiring him/her to appeal before the Magistrate and show cause why he should not be required to remove himself from the place and be prohibited from re-entering it. The Courts have invariably held this Section to be reasonable and considered it necessary to deport commercial sex workers in the interest of public health and public morals.

Besides the recommended amendments, the medical profession as well as the legal profession need to be sensitized so that they do not exploit the women on the grounds of assisting them. Legalization therefore is not the solution. In the Indian context when girls/women face so many social evils such as rape, dowry etc., the legalization of prostitution will add an additional pressure especially from families who are in dire economic straits. In addition it will support a patriarchal and dehumanizing institution which legitimizes sexual violence and enslavement.

INTERVENTIONS AND DIRECTIONS

On one hand the challenge has been : how to mobilize concerted action at the local, national and international levels so as to articulate the outrage experienced at the sexual exploitation of women and girl-children in the nation? And on the other: how to lend solidarity to a group of marginalised and alienated women and girl children who are sold into bondage in some form or the other?

The need to mobilize for concerted action arises from the fact that commercial sexual exploitation of women and girl children is largely due to criminality, particularly the fact that criminals and criminal networks perpetrate crimes against women and children. This is further exacerbated by ineffective legal strictures, lax law enforcement and limited sensibilisation of the personnel of law enforcement to deal with the issue.

While some laws, policies and programmas do exist to counter the commercial sexual exploitation of women and children, greater political will, more effective implementation measures and adequate increased allocation of resources are needed to fulfill the spirit and letter of these laws and policies.

The obligation to be in solidarity with the women who have been cheated, forced into sex-work and who find themselves at the edge of society is also very strong.

If these persons are treated with a social stigma, due to no fault of their own how do we as citizens rectify the crime committed because of the strong patriarchal tones in our society? Criminalizing and alienating this section of society in no way responds to the challenge that this issue places before us as individual, as NGOs and government agencies.

In this context the personal and organization interventions of the Joint Women's Programme and the Indian Social Institute initially assisted by a group of activist who worked towards :

Providing relevant services-medical, psychological, legal and other related services—with particular attention to STD/HIV—in as many brothels as possible with the assistance of government (LNJP/MAMC) and a few voluntary doctors.

Educating in collaboration with MAMC doctors and a voluntary doctor- Dr. J.P. Jain—on the rights of women and children and on the use of preventive methods - the use of condoms etc.—so as to avoid contacting STD/HIV.

Making available legal assistance in case of police harassment, in difficult circumstances and other alleged violations of the law.

Initiated a platform for solidarity amongst the women by conducting meetings amongst the women and the brothel keepers and sporadically the police of the area also. This platform has been named Maashal Mahila Sangathan.

Initiating communications with the controlling agents, the police, and concerned NGOs, providing information for the women through slide presentations, booklets, documentary, their children and also all of society

Promoting responsible attitudes and behavior patterns—particularly in the aspect of drug/alcohol intake—thus consequently promoting a sense of self-esteem.

Critically collaborating with the government, other concerned NGOs and Activist groups—especially the AIDS Bhedbhav Virodhi Andolan—so as to formulate policies that would benefit the women and children at risk.

During the demolition of the Babri Masjid, the writers stayed in solidarity with the women of G.B. Road all through the time of curfew and riots in the city providing medical care and counseling services.

Regular services in counseling on a weekly basis for women who needed assistance was provided at the Centre and within the brothels.

Conducting a 12 hour creche/day-care centre facilities which was initially in collaboration with the Ministry of Welfare, Government of India and now entirely the responsibility of the Joint Women's Programme, for the children of the women involved in this profession—on G.B. Road itself as also a nursery school for those above the age of 3 years. The day-care centre also coaches children attending government/private schools and who come to the centre after regular school hours.

Assisting in the admissions of children of sex-workers, in collaboration with educations, into boarding/day schools around Delhi and in States so as to provide other alternatives in their lives, especially in the lives of girls.

Presenting at all the times the viewpoint of the women themselves—at meetings, sensitize, national consultations etc. —so as to help sensitize the public and government agencies about the struggles of the women concerned, their plight and the need to plan concrete measures for rehabilitation and reintegration.

Assisting in obtaining necessary documents such as ration and I-cards and enlisting the women in the voters list.

Raising awareness amongst the sex-workers in local/ national issues around AIDS/Women by encouraging them to attend meetings, seminars, protest rallies and other programmes sponsored by both government and NGO agencies.

CONCLUSION

The red light areas of Delhi have evolved into a highly efficient business and is disciplined by harmonious controlling agents. These agents are in charge of payoffs to police, control money lending, maintain internal law and order and procure women through the vast network stretching from South India to the neighboring countries of Nepal and Bangladesh.

FUTURE DIRECTIONS

Signification compounds discovered in the course are :

Despite the fact that socio-economic and domestic factors have driven most of the women on G.B. Road into this profession as a their earnings invariably not only supports themselves but also their parents, brothers, sisters, their "so-called husband" and their own children.

Women in this profession in Delhi's G.B. Road work under different structures that range from within their families and homes to relatively independent structures or what is commonly known as the "red-light areas".

These women who are struggling to survive are treated like criminals and convicted under false charges and invariably denied their rights to genuine representation and justice.

The onset the AIDS pandemic has intensified the discrimination of these women. They are targeted as "high risk group" even though statistics show that these women are disease free prior to entry into the profession.

The Prevailing realities, attitudes and social structures marginalize the sex-workers and do not place any viable alternative offered by NGOs or the Government for a different future.

HEALTH

The health care for women in commercial sex work has been a double edged sword. The onslaught of AIDS and the various illness contracted because of their constant labour, the unhealthy environment in which they are relegated to—especially on the G.B. Road—constitutes a thread to their lives. The threat of STD/HIV+ puts them at risk from their work, and in addition they are often blamed for the spread of AIDS, whether or not they play a significant role in its transmission.

Furthermore, because they are sex-workers their needs are rarely considered that includes the need for safer working noninfected with HIV and can no longer work.

In this context alternatives such as :

Government doctors and pars—medical staff be given an orientation a sensitive approach to these women when dealing with them and where it is possible facilities need to be extended so that maximum amount of women can have these services made available to them.

Preventive care for STD/HIV in form of good quality condoms or health education needs to be planned and handled qualitatively. The Government hospitals need to work towards sensitive access to medical care for these women. Also drugs not available at Government hospitals ought to be made available for the improvement of their health conditions.

LAW

Concrete measures to check child sex-workers was discussed in May 1996 at a high-level meeting convened in the National Human Rights Commission (NHRC). The NHRC strongly endorsed stricter enforcement of laws, award of stringent punishment particularly for pimps, brothel-keepers and mafia dons, making the changes among the customers, sensitizing and motivating the policy, creation of a nodal agency with statutory powers on the lines of the Narcotics Control Bureau, galvanizing and coordinating the work of existing agencies, etc.

In offering viable alternatives in the aspect of the law, it is critical that the laws relating to sex-workers not be used against them but against their exploiters—the controlling agents. In this context the NHRC has taken a good direction. However, follow-up to these measures will be important so that they do not lie only on paper.

The participants of the NHRC high level meeting were unanimous in their feeling that economic distress, starvation, desertion by spouses and a section of the police were among the factors responsible for sex-work in the city. On the one hand, the women—especially at Delhi's G.B. Road have been forced to offer their bodies by traffickers and other controlling agents and on the other police lock them up in exploitative institution in the name of rehabilitation.

The status of Nari Niketan in 1981 indicates a starvation diet, no proper clothes, inmates not trained to earn living, forms of bonded labour and a continuation of commercial sex work (extracted from the Delhi Nari Niketan—Protection Worse Than Imprisonment. Manushi Vol. 10 1982).

The women of G.B. Road who were arrested and kept in Nari Niketan in March 1990 concurred with the above study as they recounted the sub-humane conditions at Nari Niketan. The women narraed the stage of the bathroom and the latrines which were over flowing with humane excrete and the fact that there was only one bathroom and one latrine for inmates of all age groups. They further stated that small children had sours and boils and were seen beaten by the Ayas. Hygiene was not provided for these children and food sparsely meeted out. The children hair were not oiled or cleaned and were full of lies. The women felt that the governments offer of rehabilitation was indeed a worse place than the brothels they were supposedly rescued from. These accounts of the women indicate that the women are often treated worse than criminals and provided sub-human living conditions. Naina Kapoor - a noted lawyer of Delhi—once remarked at a conference held in Delhi in 1995 that "Prostitution is not the issue, it is the people who use the women and children that are the issue." She further stated that "the definition of sexual assault in our laws is very narrow and not enough is being done to arrest the clients who are the exploiters."

In this the law-enforcing mechanism :

Needs to consider the phenomenon of commercial sex work as a socio-legal and human problem. There needs to be stronger penal measures meted out to persons involved in the procurement of girls and consideration/sensitivity offered to girls who become victims of circumstances.

A report on the meeting conduced by the National Commission of Women in January 1996 stated that 75% of the women were arrested under charges of vagrancy while a significant number were wrongfully charged with possession harassment, physical violence and extortion. The police often come without uniforms impersonating customers to arrest the women, in the process they exploit the women, threaten their children and subject them to filthy abuse and rob them of their goods. Women constables are often more violent and in human.

To combat these abuses, the law enforcers need to be sensitized given training on how to deal with the NGOs/ social workers of the area for better results. Also better treatment of young children and infants must be highlighted especially during the time when the women are placed under detention.

For the women to be better informed about the law, their own participation in illegal acts, free legal education needs to be provided. This education will assist the women to fight against the injustices meted out by the pimps/ brothel owners and other controlling agents.

Women who are harassed by the police, and have false charges framed against them should be offered free legal aid.

Legalization is definitely not a viable alternative according to the writer. Legalization of sex-workers is based primarily on an patriarchal assumption that the male sexual drive is uncontrollable and that commercial sex-workers are of that category of women set aside to give rein to this aspect of male sexuality.

This system of law, furthermore, reveals the double standards or male sexual morality because it accepts and legitimizes prostitution in society on one hand and ironically tries to maintain an appearance of false morality by cleaning up visible street prostitution. Another aspect of the encouragement of legalization of the spread of STD/AIDS an not the preservation of the health and dignity of the women.

The experience of countries that have legalized prostitution ravel that restrictions on business hours and activity spaces of sex workers and the requirement to register their movement and freedom. In addition, police harassment of these women gets heightened with legalization as through this process they are empowered to identify sex-workers for compulsory medical examinations.

EDUCATION

The most important responses that could be made by NGOs and government agencies in the field of education is good educational facilities for the children of the women in the flesh trade. Mainstream society rejects these children who through no fault of theirs survive in the situation they are forced to live in. Many of the women felt that their children were highly discriminated against in the existing educational structure in particular and in society in general. Even those who secure admission in mainstream educational institutions have to hide their identity in order for their children not to be stigmatized. High powered and good standard of education for these children will help to remove the discrimination attached to these children and provide them with alternatives other than what their mothers expose them to in the brothels.

SOCIAL ATTITUDES

In viewing the problem of prostitution, a change of social attitudes needs to happen so that the women are not marginalised and instead given an opportunity to reorient their lives and profession. The following are some possible alternatives.

Rehabilitation schemes need to be worked out with the social agencies for better directions for these women. This will be effective rather than after exploitation and abuse the women are returned to the same venue and profession.

Women should be provided with housing facilities and possible income generating activities initiated amongst them so as to move them out of the profession.

Gainful employment schemes for the women and their adolescent children especially girls.

Regular meetings with the police, State Commission Women, NGO/Government officials for representation.

Empowerment programmes so that the women gain confidence to assert themselves and make themselves heard. This will encourage their participation in political and other representative processes that can ensure their rights.

Schemes for women after the age of 40 years when they are unable to earn a living and are often physically incapacitated and condemned as destitute. If this scheme is implemented trafficking of other young women can be deterred. Social recognition and protection of women in this work. Finally facilities like ration card, travel concession for the senior citizens, pension schemes, loans etc.

THE ROLE OF NGOS

The NGO role has become a pattern of speech. The chosen rhetoric is that the NOGs are the closest to the target groups, that the NGO role is the critical one. One wonders if this is a way of transferring responsibility from one sector to another. The government cannot escape its responsibility. NGOs can be partners in government's efforts, not substitutes. There is a need to raise public sensitivity to these problems that confront us in our society.

When one closely scrutinizes the definition of NGOs, it is obvious that NGOs must include sections of media, law women's groups, academicians. This network must be broadly based to accomplish anything noteworthy. If then this network comprises NGOs how is it that very few mandates have emerged from this group in regard to women in prostitution? Are NGOs afraid to take stronger initiatives for fear that in the process of mandates, education and rehabilitation schemes they too will suffer social stigma?

A lack of coordination amongst NGOs is also a problem. Many of the NGOs in Delhi especially are keen to build their own boundaries and not open the gates to others for effective networking in fear of being hijacked in the process. Isolation is not the answer to this problem. Rather a spirit of cooperation is essential for effectivity.

SOME NGO INITIATIVES

A general feeling prevails amongst NGO groups today that the key factor in preventing girl-children from falling prey to commercial sex work is the rigid enforcement of compulsory primary education. In most states the absence of a Compulsory Education Act is an indicator of how little priority the states accord to education. If the Compulsory Education Act is not endorsed, other Acts pertaining to child labour, factories, shops and establishments, and in our context the laws pertaining to the sexual exploitation of children are reduced to a mere farce. Education, however, must be accompanied by awareness on this issue and on all levels.

The problems of child prostitution must be tackled jointly by social workers, police and the government. The village level gram sabhas must be made the focal point of prevention and rehabilitation. Gram Panchayats must be given more powers to grow into key institutions for addressing the issue of child prostitution. The government must ensure that its focus is not only on the university at the primary levels of education but on the monitoring of teachers at all levels especially in the rural areas where trafficking of children is a major concern. A task force comprising school teachers, anganwadi workers, nurses, midwives, health workers, NGOs and government officials need to be sensitized to the issue so that they can effectively educate and address the issues on the family level.

At the NGO Fourth World Conference on Women in Beijing in 1995 the issue of trafficking was discussed at great length and most of the participants were of the opinion that women who are victims of trafficking should be given the option of making their home in he country (their own or the one they are trafficked to for commercial reasons) of their choice. Governments need to assist in rehabilitating these persons and help in integrating them into new culture and environment.

In conclusion we state that the following measures are essential :

NATIONAL LEVEL

Attractive employment opportunities in viable enterprises within the rural areas as an alternatives to out-migration need to be worked through and created as soon as possible;

Discouragement of the recruitment of young girls into prostitution by disseminating among the rural population information describing the realities of the prostitution trade;

Provision of information and counseling to young women intending to work abroad and an access to persons/centres that will facilitate the process of understanding this exploitative trade;

Raising of the level of effectiveness of law enforcement against the procurers and organizers of forced prostitution;

Ratification and implement ITPP Act and the Exploitation of the Prostitution of Others.

REGIONAL LEVEL

To assist in the establishment of a regional network of NGOs and governmental agencies and concerned citizens to per cent sex trafficking and its links with drug trafficking through research, information collection and dissemination and concerted action on social and economic to aspects of prostitution and other factors cotributing to the exploitation and sexual abuse of women.

INTERNATIONAL LEVEL

To evolve strategies that will strengthen the collaboration between the action groups in the developing countries and the concerned groups in the developed countries to curb the translational dimension of tourism-related prostitution and the exploitation of female migrant workers especially of tribal and dalit women;

To prevent the sexual abuse and exploitation of young girls from developing countries through practices such as the mail order bride system by urging Interpol, among others, to undertake effective and systematic must pressurize tourist and social agencies to fully support these efforts.

To urge government and voluntary action groups to call on international networks of national law enforcement agencies to focus special attention on preventing of those involved in the trafficking in women;

Recommendations for rehabilitation of former sex-workers :

COMMUNITY LEVEL

To establish drop-in centres that provide commercial sex workers and other sexually abused and exploited women with support and friendship :

RESEARCH ACTIVITIES

To monitor and evaluate policies and programmes that encourage sexual exploitation example related to tourism.

To study the situation of vulnerable young women in urban areas and to:

(a) Formulate policies and programmes for the overall development and employment of young women;

(b) Introduce protective measures for young women workers with regard to the nature of employment, working conditions and terms of remuneration;

(c) Examine the role of media in creating and maintaining a demand for sex-workers through pornography;

(d) To review labour legislation: for possible loopholes that make young women workers vulnerable and insecure thus precipitating their entry into prostitution;

(e) To review existing laws with a view to decriminalizing prostitution as a means of protection for and to facilitate the rehabilitation of young women;

Personal findings and research indicate that women, at the local level, have become more aware of the problem and are wiling to take action against trafficking. However, more accurate information and appropriate counseling in implementing actions, at all levels, is important to prevent migrant trafficking. Initiatives and participation of women in organized campaigns need to be promoted along with national and international networking. All these measures must seriously be taken so as to combat the sexual enslavery of women at all levels.

Caution against the separation of women from children on the issue of trafficking is important. There are strong links with this type of trafficking, sex tourism and the mail order bride industries, both of which are forms of prostitution of women and children. The issues concerning children cannot be separated from those concerning women; women and children are closely related entities.

Whatever by the social compulsion under which women sex-workers come to the profession, society must bear in mind that they are not commodities in the market. The study highlights the helpless and economic situation of women in the flesh trade, women left at the mercy of "brokers, pimps and other controlling agents" The sexual exploitation of these women is our national shame.

Countries of destination and countries of origin should cooperate in providing information to each other on the causes and consequences of migration and the recommendations they may be confronted with constantly. States should supervise agencies offering overseas, employment, especially with regard to the informal sector. NGOs can play an important role in this respect.

An examination of the socio-cultural structures which makes, the present continuing supply and demand for trafficking possible, should be done and countries of origin and destination should take steps to rectify structures wherever any whenever necessary. Women are important to all nations, therefore, planing of strategies and implementing them accordingly will manifest the importance of women kind. The Challenge is Ours.

THE BUSINESS TRAVELLER

Those who travel for business rather than pleasure share many of the attributes listed above. However, they are often more sophisticated travellers and usually have more money to spend. Some of them are more likely to remain in one place for long periods, others return often to the same place. Business people usually travel alone and are largely male. Not surprisingly, a number of serious cases of consistent commercial child exploitation have been uncovered among travelling men in the business community.

BUSINESS PEOPLE WITHIN POOR COUNTRIES

On the other hand, business people in poor countries where tourists arrive in greater numbers, see and seize opportunities for substantial profit at low risk and little investment by developing a sex industry, using the available prostitutes, enticing or forcing women to get involved, and if necessary, recruit or force children to become .sex-workers.. The sex industry is organised like most other industries. It is a sector in which individuals as well as large organisations operate. It frequently has connections with other illegal and exploitative behaviour - such as trafficking of children, forced labour and pornography.

5

SEX TOURISM IN WORLD

INTRODUCTION

The sex services industry has been expressed by local patriotic and church women's groups in the host countries. Some westerners have viewed the phenomenon with interest because it seems even more exotic than other popular images of Asia and Asian cultures. Moreover, the group behaviour of Japanese male sex tourists strikes many Americans and Europeans as odd, even comical. But the real significance of sex tourism is political and economic as well as cultural: sex tourism reflects the unequal political and economic relationship between developing and industrialized nations and between the sexes on a worldwide scale.

The continued economic gap between many nations in East and Southeast Asia and the wealthy nations in the West and Japan a gap resulting from decades of war and colonial rule, makes the most valued commodity in South Korea, Taiwan, Hong Kong, and the Philippines continue to be low-wage skilled, semi-skilled, and unskilled labour in foreign controlled industries. Asia supplies workers, whether as immigrants or as temporary contract labourers, to Western Europe, Australia, the U.S. and, more recently, the Middle East. As demand for travel and recreation facilities increases in industrialized counties, expanding the market for exporters of human labour, are now vying with one another to market sex and sexual services to the developed world.

Prostitution tourism in Asia today is multinational. The sellers are from Taiwan, South Korea, Thailand, and the Philippines, Indonesia, Malaysia, Sri Lanka—wherever there exists a largely unskilled and needy female labour force and local governments that are searching for even short-range solutions to foreign exchange problems in their shaky economies. The buyers are from Europe, Australia, the United States, and Japan where rising individual incomes and their often shady procurers, protectors, and employers, it also involves their staunchly middle-class customers from Japan and the West Not could the vast enterprises exist without the active participation of Japanese, European, and local travel and tour agencies, multinational hotel chains, airline companies, and local government offices that promote and maintain this industry.

CREATING FORCES

The Asian colonial where sex tourism is practised have faced decades of war and colonial rule. "The century of murderous war in Asia began with the U.S. colonial war in the Philippines, was followed by Japan's half century of invasion, colonization and war with Asia, by successive U.S. wars from the U.S.—Japan Pacific War to Korea and Vietnam and a host of anti-colonial wars and revolutions. It came to an end in the year 2000 with East Timor's independence ending Indonesia's 25-year pogrom. All of these wars are notable for the targeting of non-combatants in general and violence against women in particular" (Mark Selden).

War impoverishes countries. Many Southeast Asian nations are still recovering from the devastation of war. According to statistics published by BOND—a non-governmental organization in the UK—in September 2002,

Asia is the home of over seventy-five per cent of the world's poor, forty per cent live in South Asia alone, living on the equivalent of less than one U.S. dollar a day. The sexploitation of the women and children is evident in history; it has been initiated and left behind by jarring wars and colonialism, both of which have contributed to large economic gaps between Third World countries and their industrial neighbours.

The misfortunes of the women and children affected by the sex industry are caused by desperation: a need to eat, a need to clothe their younger siblings, and to care for their ailing parents. The skeleton framework of a Third World Country's economy causes this desperation. Without available jobs or a welfare system to support the dirt-poor constituents of these countries, the women and children become forcibly employed in degrading work.

According to Elaine Kirn's "Sex Tourism in Asia," the so-called sellers of the demanding sex industry are countries (some of which are Taiwan, Thailand, South Korea, the Philippines) who have "a largely unskilled and needy female labour force and local governments that are searching for even short-range solutions to foreign exchange problems in their shaky economies".

Governments have no choice but to turn a blind eye, or even encourage prostitution in order to increase their domestic gross product. Governments that declare prostitution as illegal hypocritically promote it.

In the Philippines, a government-financed hotel named the Ramada, hotel visitors are handed sheets that have rules about how to go about "ordering" their women. Similarly, South Korean government supports travel tours that offer these packages, "Four days and three nights, including round trip air fare, hotel accommodations, meals and a woman for each night for only $ 615" (Kim, 220).

STATISTICS

Asia alone has 1 million women sold into prostitution each year 1993 and 1994 estimates for the number prostitutes *via* country's reports submitted to the International Labour Organization (ILO) Reference #2 Unknown. "Sex industry assuming massive proportions in Southeast Asia." Vol. 24, WIN News, 09-22-1998, pp 65 (1). Date of access: 4/5/03, http://ask.elibrary.com/. Indonesia 140,000-230,000 numbers are higher according to the ILO Malaysia 43,000-142,000 numbers are higher according to the ILO Philippines 100,000-600,000 with a half million in the country Thailand 65,000 from the Ministry of Public Health + 200,000-300,000 by 1997 unofficial sources Several million people are involved in the sex trade within these countries if you include owners, managers, pimps and other employees that earn a monetary living directly or indirectly from prostitution. Reference #3 Unknown. "Trafficking in Women and Prostitution in the Asia Pacific: Part One." Contemporary Women's Issues Database, 01-01-1997. Date of access: 4/5/03, http://ask.elibrary.com/. 1970 Post-war prosperity in Northern countries gave purchasing power and new forms of sex commerce that glamorized porn because of the demand 1991 incident of kidnapped women at the Pakistan-Afghan border, these women were to be sold into the marketplace (for Rs. 600 per kilogram). 1991 Filipino, Thai, and Taiwanese women sold in Japan for $2,400-$18,000 each and resold by the Japanese promoter to other sex business owners at double the price, the women could also be rented for $1,600-$6,400 monthly charge. The women may receive a small percentage as commission, normally only after she repays the expenses of the passport and travel papers.

Laws/Attempt at Control Unknown. "Prostitution." The Columbia Encyclopaedia, Seventh Edition, 01-01-2002. Date of access: 4/5/03, http://ask.elibrary.com/. Europe 16th

Century brothels were closed throughout Western and Central Europe and punishment to those engaged in the trade was unsuccessful 1700 Berlin—medical inspections 1785 Paris registered prostitutes Great Britain Legislation—Contagious Diseases Prevention Acts of 1864, 1866 and 1869 were enacted to control the spread of Sexually Transmitted Diseases (STD), required periodic medical exams to prostitutes. Failed to control disease and was repealed in 1886, 1898 Vagrancy Act prohibited males from living on earnings of prostitutes.

United States 1910 Mann Act (efforts of James Robert Mann) aka the White Slave Traffic Act—forbade under severe penalty interstate and international transport of women for immoral purposes 1915. Nearly all states had laws regarding keeping brothels or otherwise profiting from prostitutes earnings WWI increase in prostitution parallel the STD increase 1941 Congress made the May Act because of the rise in STDs near military bases. Made practising prostitution a federal offence in areas designated by Army and Navy Secretaries Laws have been enacted in all states for all forms of prostitution (except Nevada)—while customers are often exempt from prosecution Current legislation concerns with the removal of crimes associated with prostitution, the spread of AIDS revised the discussion in US International Late 19th Century began the efforts to control 1899 began with conferences with Congress in London, 1901 Amsterdam, and 1902 London 1904 Paris conference came to an international resolution to provide for specific agency in each nation to suppress prostitution 1919 League of Nations appointed an official body to gather all facts about trafficking of prostitution 1921 Geneva Conference with 34 countries established the Committee on the Traffic in Women and Children, work was taken over by the United Nations in 1946-1949 convention for the suppression of prostitution adopted by the UN General Assembly British Parliamentary Act of 1959 permits prostitution or other forms of sexual conduct within homes by consenting adults, forbidding open solicitation. Not a punishable crime within adults, and if the prostitute ever wants to quit there are rehabilitation centers where they can be taught commercial or technical skills. Netherlands, Germany and other countries emphasize hygienic aspects within legislation, rigidly enforcing periodic medical exams and gives free hospitalization for those found infected. Regulation rather than suppression has led to the decline in STDs and removes bribery of law enforcement officers.

Philippines Cost of sex tour package: $1,645 per person includes round trip airfare, hotel, guided tours to sex bars (Philippine Adventure Tours). The Gross Domestic Product (GDP) earns 2-14% of its revenue from sex trafficking. The financial gains are crucial to the livelihood and earnings of millions of workers, *i.e.*,—tour agencies, escort services, hotel room service, sauna and health clinics. Filipino overseas contract workers earn a billion dollars that keeps the economy afloat for 2 decades now. Government turns a blind eye during cases of abuse and claim they are isolated cases because they do not want to upset "delicate foreign relations, especially regional ties.

Thailand 1997 Ministry of Public Health of Thailand study of 1,04,262 workers within 7,759—establishments/ sex services. Of the above reported numbers 64,886 are sex workers, the remaining are support staff (cleaners, waiters, cashiers, parking valets and security guards) (1). Brothel networks have a rotation system that keeps victims perpetually in debt because a girl is resold just before her debt is fully paid to the first brothel-hence her balance to free herself begins at a zero payment to the second brothel (2). After debts can be paid off most women must stay within the brothel circuit to earn a living. Thai women sold to Australia are given the illusion they will be waitresses, but are given a false passport and travel documents to get them to a brothel where they must pay off a $ 15,000 debt Brothels and other sexual service centers have an estimated 50,000 establishments. Approximately 1 million women are trafficked into Thailand because they do not speak the common language. 50% of these prostitutes are from the remote jungles in the remote North Burmese jungles and are "beautified" before they are sold into prostitution (3). Women from Thailand are able to move back home after prostitution. Bangladeshi women fear and risk being killed by their own families (4).

Australia Unknown. "Trafficking in Women and Prostitution in the Asia Pacific: Part One." Contemporary Women's Issues Database. 01-01-1997. Date of access: 4/5/03, http://ask.elibrary.com/. Trafficked women begin with a debt of $15,000-$18,000 and only after approximately 200 customers, at $45 each, the women are able to start earning a living for themselves. Sydney Sexual Health Centre claims many women work in pain and with active infections, pelvic inflammatory diseases, acute herpes, and traumatic pelvic syndromes. All as a result from pressure to serve clients and be able to pay off their bonds as soon as possible. Australian Federal Police established in 1988 that illegal prostitution was grossing A$30 million a year. Filipinas were once the predominant sex trafficked women, now Thais and Malaysians are increasing in numbers along with the Indonesian increase to Australia.

India Debt forces Nepalese and Bangladeshi women to work long hours and have more clients than local women (3). Most work without condoms and undercut prices to get enough clients Bangladeshi women/victims are seen as "fallen" or "undeserving." Some trafficking has been influenced by technology, but 74 Bangladeshi women and children were recently sold to Pakistan and were rescued from the cargo hold of a boat as they were bound and gagged. Sixty per cent of prostituted women suffer from

STDs and AIDS in Bombay's red light district and only sent home as they are about to die (4).

ADVERTISING

There are two primary approaches used in sex advertising for tourism: amount of nudity and degree of suggestiveness. The amount of nudity directly relates to the image displayed. Suggestiveness, on the other hand, can relate either to the image, such as a provocative pose or couples walking down a beach, or it can relate to the language used in the advertisement. It is often a powerful motivator because language works alongside with the imagery used and in some cases, both elements obtain their meaning only when used together.

SEX AND INNUENDO

Nudity and innuendo have always been a part in advertising as a way to increase awareness and attention to a particular advertisement. Sex is used in advertising because it is a persuasive motivator in consumer behaviour. Typically, sex advertising takes two forms. The first is language promotional, which describes the destination and its people in sexually permissive terms, thus actually location erotic feelings in a potential tourist. The second in sexual mythology, which plays on commonly held popular beliefs about a certain race.

OUTCOME

Advertising presents an unrealistic or idealized picture of people and their lives. By using attractive models, advertisements invite a social comparison of the viewers with these models, which may result in lower self-satisfaction among viewers, despite being aware of the unrealistic nature of the advertisements. Furthermore, the advertising works! The reality of these campaigns is that they are extremely effective in prompting men to purchase these trips and serve as the lifeblood of the industry.

DEMAND

This quote from a sex tour company is one of the main incentives for men who take part in sex tour packages. Asian women are in high demand and therefore marketable due to a reaction to the stereotypes which surround them, the white women's feminist movement, as well as a backlash against it and the social and psychological needs of the men who partake in such activities.

Because of the economic discrepancy between the countries the men come from and the Third World countries where they go, it is much cheaper to have a woman in other countries. This allows the men to feel dominant over the women. This need for psychological dominance ties into the appeal of the stereotype of the Asian woman as a submissive "geisha" type. This image of a subordinate woman is what is being marketed. Asian women are seen as knowing how to cater to a man and please whomever they are serving, as opposed to American women, who have been too educated and "brainwashed" by feminist propaganda. The sex tourism operators all use similar themes of Asia being a sexual playground for American men. They perpetuate the notion that all Asian women are willing, docile and adoring.

Big Apple Tours emphasizes this, boasting of how "In Asia you'll meet girls who will treat you with respect and appreciation, unlike their American counterparts." A letter from one young Japanese in Jitsuwa to Hiroku inquiring about South Korean "services" for men received the following reply, "There are only two types of people who don't sleep with South Korean women: those with no money and those with something wrong with a certain part of their body... [Besides being] rather cheap... those Korean girls are... all between 18 and 25 and very ripe [with]... tight purses.

(Taken from Elaine Kim's Sex Tourism in Asia: A Reflection of Political and Economic Inequality). This stereotype has created an industry where a woman's body is a marketable commodity, and "a woman's ability to please a man is a measure of her ability to earn her living well"

CHILD PROSTITUTION AND SEX TOURISM—GOA

Child sexual exploitation is not a new phenomenon in Goa. In particular, the sexual exploitation of female child prostitutes has a long history. Goa's red light districts are by no means recently established and the children prostituted there have, in the past, served a clientele predominantly made up of local men, migrant workers and sailors. It also seems probable that a trickle of foreign demand for prostituted children has existed for a long time.

Under Portugese colonial rule, such children were no doubt sexually exploited by colonial officials and administrators as well as by 'curious' foreign visitors. It also seems unlikely that the presence of foreign paedophiles in Goan society is entirely new.

Colonial domination has invariably involved the sexual exploitation of vulnerable children and women as well as the political subjection and economic exploitation of a people.

However, there is reason to believe that the numbers of sexual exploiters in Goa are now swelling as a result of both domestic and foreign tourism. The tourist industry in India has expanded rapidly since the 1980s and is now the country's largest single foreign exchange earner.

Investment in tourism has been explicitly promoted by the Government which offers a series of incentives to national and multinational capital (Suresh, 1995).

Goa, with its great natural beauty, pleasant climate and distinctive history of Portugese colonial rule has been one of the key foci of this national and international investment. As a foreign exchange earner, tourism is often assumed to yield significant benefits for 'Third World' countries.

Whether it actually does bring net economic benefits is a matter of dispute (see Ferguson, 1990, and Pattullo, 1996, on the effects of tourist development on local economies in the Caribbean, for example) but what is certain is that tourist development has a number of extremely negative environmental and social consequences in poor countries.

In particular, many regions of the economically underdeveloped world which have had tourism foisted upon them by world financial institutions and international capital have found themselves fast becoming centres of various forms of sexual tourism and child sexual exploitation.

In some cases, tourism has served to maintain and develop the country's existing formal sex industry. In others, tourism has been more strongly associated with the emergence of new and more informal types of prostitution.

Our aim in this report is threefold: to describe the various different contexts in which children are sexually exploited in Goa; to examine the identity and motivations of those who exploit them; and to discuss the risk of western package tourism turning into mass western sex tourism in Goa.

We begin with a discussion of the methodological problems encountered during fieldwork in Goa and these are problems which readers must keep in mind throughout the remainder of the report.

METHODOLOGICAL PROBLEMS AND ISSUES

Fieldwork in Goa was undertaken by Julia O'Connell Davidson and Jacqueline Sanchez Taylor in January 1999, and the data upon which this report is based has several limitations.

First, it was collected over a very short period of time. Since we had only eight days and nights in which to work, there were many 'leads' which we were unable to pursue and many places we were unable to visit.

Second, the most numerically significant group of sex tourists in Goa are domestic tourists from other parts of India and since we did not have the language skills necessary to interview them, we have no direct data on this key group of exploiters.

Third, because western sex tourists are not present in Goa in large numbers, the sample of sex tourists available to observe and interview was very small.

Fourth, because females in Goa are either prostituted in red light districts which are geographically separated from tourist resorts or are prostituted in an extremely clandestine way in tourist resorts, it was impossible for us to adopt our normal research strategy of immersing ourselves in the environments in which women and girls work, interviewing them and observing them interact with clients. We spent a long afternoon in a red light district where we were able to talk to some prostituted women and children as well as to one pimp but the data from such a brief visit is in no way comparable in depth or richness to that which we usually obtain by spending several days and nights constantly working in such environments.

Finally, the children who are most vulnerable to sexual exploitation in Goa do not usually speak more than a smattering of English and since neither of us speak even a word of their various mother-tongues it was very difficult for us to conduct the kind of delicate interview that is necessary to draw information from child victims of sexual abuse.

We were lucky on three different occasions to meet Karnatak children who spoke very good English and were able to tell us extremely disturbing stories about the activities of western tourists in Goa, but on the whole our interview work with such children was frustrating and inconclusive.

It was impossible to tell whether they had fully understood our questions and equally impossible to be certain whether we understood their replies.

In all, we managed to conduct in-depth interviews (one hour plus) with five Macho Lad sex tourists, two aging hippy sex exploiters and one suspected paedophile expatriate as well as short interviews (less than one hour) with four prostitute—using sailors, three more Macho Lad sex tourists and two more 'sexpatriate' hippies. We attempted to compensate for this very small sample in the following ways:

- by interviewing prostitutes in the red light district we visited and beach sellers who are vulnerable to sexual exploitation;
- by interviewing tourists who were not sexual exploiters about their experiences, observations and attitudes;
- by interviewing shopkeepers, bar owners and hotel staff about their observations of tourist behaviour.

We were extremely fortunate to be offered assistance by the Jagrut Goenkaranchi Fouz (JGF) and we are especially indebted to Caroline Colaso who took us to a red light district, introduced us to a group of nuns working with the children of sex workers and guided us around what would otherwise have been an inaccessible area.

We are also fortunate to be in a position to consider and compare interview material from sex tourists and sexpatriates in Goa against that obtained from a far greater sample of such men collected on research trips to Thailand, Cuba, Costa Rica, the Dominican Republic and Venezuela, something which we believe makes the analysis provided below more reliable, despite being based on a small sample.

We hope, then, that despite all of the methodological problems we faced, we can provide some insight into the identity and motivations of western sexual exploiters in Goa.

What we cannot do, and it is important for the reader to keep this clearly in mind when assessing the information provided in this report, is to provide reliable information about the scale of the problem of child sexual exploitation in Goa.

Playing the numbers game in relation to child sexual abuse is, as Ennew (1986) observes, a particularly repugnant activity. It should not be necessary to demonstrate that x hundred or x thousand children are affected before the national Government and international community are prepared to act. But it is also important not to exaggerate the scale of the phenomenon. It is as irresponsible to publicise claims that a given country or resort is a 'paedophile paradise' as it is to deny the existence of the problem of child sexual exploitation.

Our research was concerned to discover the forms which the sexual exploitation of children can take in Goa and to explore the motivations and attitudes of western men who practice sex tourism and child sexual abuse there. It did not attempt to measure the extent of the problem nor to produce numerical data on the numbers of sex tourists and expatriates involved in the sexual exploitation of children in Goa.

SEXUAL ACCESS TO CHILDREN IN GOA

As is the case in many other parts of the world, sexual access to children can be attained in several different ways in Goa. These are considered below.

Organised Prostitution

Goa's red light districts are small by comparison to those of cities such as Bombay, Calcutta and Delhi but they share many similar features. In the red light districts of India's major cities and ports there are few, if any, local prostitutes. The majority have either migrated or been trafficked to those cities and 'trafficking in India takes place at both intra-and inter-state level' (Lalou, 1995).

It is also the case that, despite legal prohibitions on trafficking, procuring and prostituting children (Section 366 of the Indian Penal Code), a high percentage of the prostitutes working in such districts are under the age of 18. Of these, a sizeable proportion are victims of the Devadasis system and have been 'dedicated' to the Godess Yellamma (around 10,000 girls in India are dedicated annually—Alou, 1995). Goa's red light districts share these features.

Prostitutes there are typically migrants (or the children of migrants) from Karnataka, Andhra Pradesh or Maharashtra. Whether or not they are sacrificed to the Devadasis system, the daughters of migrant prostitute women are generally expected to enter into prostitution as soon as they reach puberty, signalled by the onset of menstruation.

Before this, their economic activity takes the form of begging and/or dancing in bars 'to the tunes of Hindi film songs to entertain sailors who pay them for their performance. The dances usually last between half an hour and two hours.... As soon as the dance is over, some of the children beg for money' (INSAF, 1995).

The red light area we visited in Goa consisted of a series of narrow streets, each lined with dwellings divided into small rooms which were rented by prostitutes. Dotted amongst these streets were bars and restaurants. Though our informants reported that there is little brothel based prostitution in this district, most prostitutes are controlled by pimps or *Garhwalli* (women pimps, often themselves ex-prostitutes) and there are other layers of third party involvement in prostitution.

Financial beneficiaries include the bar and restaurant owners and the renting agents, who charge prostitutes between 200 and 400 rupees per month for the unsanitary cells in which they must live and work. Some pimps play a more active role than others in soliciting custom.

Those who own motorbikes and travel outside the red light districts in search of clients are known as 'pilots'. Pimps tend to be 'kin' to the prostitutes they exploit, either their husbands or relatives, or simply in the sense of being migrants from the same region as the prostitutes whom they work.

This means that migrant prostitute women and children economically support male migrants from the same region as well as themselves and their own children.

Prices paid by clients range between 50 and 1,000 rupees, depending upon the prostitute's age and looks and the client's disposable income. The client may also pay a 'finder's fee' to the pimp or pilot, who may further demand a direct cut from the prostitute's earnings.

Prepuberlal dancing girls earn between 25 and 30 rupees plus tips for a night's work performing in bars. Research by INSAF (1995) suggests that in this single red light district alone about 1,000 children are at risk of being prostituted.

Some commentators state that a new form of organised prostitution is emerging in Goa, one which caters solely to tourist demand. Suresh (1995), for example, observes that 'It is no great secret that the number of massage parlours and health clubs that have mushroomed in Goa hotels are only fronts for organised prostitution rackets'.

We were unable to investigate this form of prostitution. None of the tourists we interviewed had encountered such prostitution, which leads us to believe that hotel prostitution in Goa is not taking place on the same scale that it is in parts of China and the former Soveit Union (hotel guests in these places report being constantly called on their room phone and approached in lifts, corridors, foyers etc., by 'masseuses' offering sexual services).

But it does not follow that there is no organised hotel prostitution in Goa, simply that we could not investigate it in the time available to us.

Informal Prostitution

As well as prostitution which takes piece within the red light districts, more informal forms of prostitution exist in Goa. These can be divided into three main types. First, there are boys and young men who independently enter into longer term sexual relationships with female, and sometimes male, tourists in exchange for economic benefits.

These are not narrowly specified, contractual transactions (x sexual service in exchange for x sum of money) and the local male will typically perform a diverse range of services for his tourist 'friend', acting as guide and companion, for example. The tourist will likewise provide a diffuse range of benefits, including meals, drinks, clothing and 'pocket money'.

Some tourist 'friends' will make very substantial gifts upon leaving Goa, a lump sum to set up business or a motorbike, and this is especially likely where the tourist has spent a period of months with the same boy.

The second type of informal prostitution involves opportunistic procuring by men who 'moonlight' as pimps rather than relying upon pimping as their sole means of subsistence.

Taxi drivers are especially prone to supplementing their income in this way. A taxi driver involved in this type of prostitution will offer to supply the tourist in his cab with a prostitute for between 300 and 600 rupees.

If the tourist agrees, the taxi driver will then deliver a prostitute to the tourist's hotel room and collect her/him the following morning. Some taxi drivers fetch the prostitute from a red light district, paying her/his pimp a small percentage of the finder's fee he has secured from the tourist.

Others appear to have a more stable arrangement with one or two women/children whom they regularly prostitute in this way. A British tourist described his encounter with a taxi driver/pimp as follows:

The taxi driver was very chatty and friendly, 'Where are you staying?', 'Do you like Goa?', that kind of thing. Then he just said: 'Do you want prostitute? I have girls, 16 or 17 years, nice girls'. I said 'No' and he was very pushy. 'Only 300 rupees' and he could bring her to the hotel, she'd spend the whole night with me. He seemed offended because I kept saying 'No'. Eventually he said, 'Or you want boy? I can find you boy'.

Third, there is evidence to suggest that some tourists are involved in a type of informal child prostitution. A large community of migrant workers, mainly from Karnataka, lives in Goa in small makeshift shanty towns (ragged tents and structures erected on the outskirts of larger towns, with no water, electricity or sanitation).

The pressure to migrate from drought-prone and poverty-stricken regions surrounding Goa is intense. Adult male migrants are usually involved in construction, stone quarrying or scrap collection work, while migrant women and children often work selling lungis, trinkets, fruit, nuts, soft drinks and so on to tourists on the beaches.

Some adults and children also sell massages to tourists. Other children collect scrap, beg around market places and/ or offer to guide tourists. The beach sellers tend to work in groups, and often this involves groups of children working all day on beaches several miles from their home, without any adult supervision.

Of necessity, their work entails approaching strangers and chatting to them in a friendly, open fashion. Such children report that male tourists have, on occasion, been extremely 'friendly' and then invited them to stay in their hotels or apartments, offering them very large sums of money for so doing (children mentioned sums of $ US 100, or 'thousands of rupees').

None of the beach seller children we interviewed admitted to having ever taken a tourist up on such an offer but several such children claimed to know other children who had done so.

They told us that children 'go with' tourists for one or two days and when they return they have 'lots of money'.

We were also told stories about children being taken out of the country by tourists for lengthy periods of time; for instance, a story about a nine years old and a six years old being taken to Europe by a German tourist who paid their parents a large amount of money and returned the boys a year later.

The same informants claimed to know another two children who are in the process of being 'bought' from their parents by an English man who wants to take them to England to live with him.

We could not substantiate such stories but the fact that several migrant beach seller children reported being offered money by single, male tourists to accompany them to their hotel rooms and apartments and knew that an economic value is attached to children by foreigners, suggests that some tourists do make informal and opportunistic arrangements to buy sexual access to children's bodies.

Sexual Abuse in Non-commercial Contexts

Some paedophiles and preferential child sex abusers seek jobs or positions which provide them with opportunities to abuse, or move to locations where they know that sexual access to children is relatively easily attained.

Certain groups of children are therefore at particular risk of sexual abuse. Street children and children in orphanages are obvious examples of children who are vulnerable to sexual abuse by adults occupying positions of trust or authority.

They are easy targets for paedophiles and preferential abusers since they are, by definition, emotionally needy and materially deprived. Adults in positions of trust or authority are therefore able to manipulate them with promises, threats and bribes, often making the child feel complicit in its own abuse.

India as a whole has the largest number of orphaned and abandoned children in the world (Singly, 1989) and although Goa is wealthy by comparison to neighbouring states like Karnataka and Maharashtra, it is not in a position to provide even the most basic support for the population of orphaned and abandoned children that live in it.

In such a context, the efforts made by apparently philanthropic individuals to 'help' children are welcomed and the motives of men who set up and run orphanages or provide shelter and employment for street children are unlikely to be interrogated too closely, as the recent trial of Freddie Peats has demonstrated only too graphically.

Between 1984 and 1991, Peats ran a boarding house-children's home, taking in orphaned boys and boys from broken homes and sexually abusing them. Peats also used the boys in the production of pornography and prostituted them to foreign paedophiles.

Yet for many years Peats remained a respected figure in the local community and his boarding house, which was not registered with the social welfare department of the State Government as it should have been, was not investigated.

It seems unlikely that the Peats case represents a single, isolated incident. Whilst in Goa we investigated, as best we could, rumours about a British expatriate running a small travel agency in North Goa.

This man surrounded himself with young boys, offering them shelter and employment and he closely conformed to the psychological profile of one type of paedophile. He organises tours to Sri Lanka from Goa and is reputed to have close links with a Catholic priest who runs a home for abandoned and orphaned children in the neighbouring town.

Subsequent to our meeting with this man, he is alleged to have confessed his abusive practices to a male investigative journalist from a British tabloid paper. The same journalist claims to have evidence that another British expatriate in the same town is involved in a paedophile ring.

The fact that a children's park in Goa was mentioned in John Stamford's Sparticus Guide as a cruising ground gives further reason to believe that some paedophiles may identify Goa as a location in which sexual access to children is a possibility.

There is another reason for arguing against the proposition that the Peats case was an isolated incident.

Paedophiles of his ilk tend to seek out the company of like-minded men. There are numerous documented cases in which such paedophiles have prostituted their victims and/ or used them in the production of pornography which is then circulated to other paedophiles.

At one level, this form of commercial sexual exploitation needs to be understood as part of the abuse perpetrated by the paedophile, who derives sexual and psychological pleasure from seeing the child degraded and objectified in this way.

Moreover, to witness other adults sexually abusing children reduces any sense of guilt or sexual isolation the paedophile may experience, and to organise and orchestrate this type of abuse gives the paedophile an immense sense of power and control. Other people—adults as well as children—become mere puppets in his theatre, and mastering others in this way makes them appear less threatening.

There are also financial incentives for paedophiles to prostitute children. Though paedophile 'sex tours' and pornography are not especially profitable commercial opportunities (the market is too small and specialised) for the individual paedophile, they can provide a means of supporting and sustaining his own abusive 'lifestyle'. Peats' activities allowed him to run his boarding house, feeding and clothing 25 boys at a time, without having any legal source of income, for example.

One paedophile can thus attract ten, twenty or thirty more to an area, of whom some may continue to visit even after their original 'host' has stopped arranging sexual access to children for them. One or two may even decide to settle in the place and in this way the numbers of abusers in a given location can increase in a gradual fashion.

If that location combines large numbers of vulnerable children, a high degree of police corruption and/or an under-resourced police force inexperienced in dealing with child sexual offences plus a high degree of respect for western men, then it will be even more attractive to paedophiles looking for places in which they can cheaply and safely satisfy their sexual interests.

SEX EXPLOITERS IN GOA

In Goa, as in many other parts of the world, local men, migrant workers and seamen represent the traditional source of demand for prostitution.

We were unable to interview any local or migrant prostitute users but did manage to briefly interview four Ukrainian sailors who admitted to using prostitutes in Goan red lights districts, as well as in Bombay, Cuba, Thailand, the Philippines and Brazil. These men were all in their late 20s and were working an eight month contract on ship, moving mainly between the Arab Emirates, India and Indonesia.

Every few months the ship stopped for seven days, during which time the men were allowed to go ashore between 8 a.m. and 6 p.m. When we interviewed them, their ship had anchored off the Goan coast. On their first day of 'rest' these four men, along with several other crew members, had come ashore and gone immediately to a red light district.

We asked them how they knew of its existence and they explained that on a previous stop in Bombay they had met a German sex tourist who told them that if they ever went to Goa this was the best spot to find 'whores'.

According to these men, the Goan red light district compared favourably to red light areas in other countries. It was extremely cheap (although they bemoaned the fact that white men have to pay more than Indian clients 'The black man pays $5, the white man has to pay $20'. For $20, however, a man 'can get everything, excellent service, anything you want'.

We asked whether some of the prostitutes were very young. 'Yes', one sailor replied. 'There's a choice of all ages. If you have money you can have anything you want here'.

These sailors were young men, all of whom were, in terms of western cultural norms, attractive and fashionably dressed.

They explained their prostitute use through reference to a belief in a biologically determined male sexual drive. As one put it, 'I'm a man, I have biological needs. I've been on ship for months, without a woman. I had to have one'.

For men like this, prostituted women and children are simply receptacles for the 'natural' impulses of men to be evacuated into. This image of human beings as nothing more than sexual latrines was further reinforced by the sailors' comments on the nature of their interaction with prostitutes. We asked whether they could, for $20, spend as long as they wanted with a girl. One replied as follows:

You could. You could spend the whole night with her. But you wouldn't want to spend more than an hour in that place. It's filthy. It's horrible. You only stay long enough for your needs. It's horrible. It's dirty. You don't go there from choice, only necessity.

Prostitute users who justify themselves through reference to a story about men having a biological need for sex and about prostitute women and children being nothing but dehumanised objects for men's urges are always looking for ways in which to bolster that story and so to defend themselves from uncomfortable truths about their own moral responsibility.

These sailors were no exception. We asked them to fill out a questionnaire which asked whether they believed that in Goa attitudes towards sexuality are more permissive, less permissive or the same as in the west.

All four men agreed that in Goa attitudes towards casual sex, homosexuality and prostitution are *more* permissive, a rather extraordinary conclusion from men who moments earlier had stated that it would be impossible for them to find a non-commercial sexual partner in India because Indians are so 'strictly religious'.

Such inconsistencies are not uncommon in the world view of sexual exploiters who serve to justify what is morally indefensible.

These men tell themselves that there is nothing reprehensible about having sex with a young girl who must live all day, every day of her life, in a hovel so filthy that they themselves would not spend any longer than 'necessary' in it. They tell themselves, it is 'their way of life out here'.

It was noted above that the majority of prostitutes working in red light districts are migrants rather than Goans. It seems likely that local prostitute users employ much the same type of 'Otherizing' to justify their sexual exploitation of prostitute women and children (difference in caste, religion and birthplace can all be used to dehumanise the prostitute) and it may well be that migrant workers do likewise.

Finally, it is important to reiterate that all the prostitute users discussed in this section are highly likely to sexually abuse children, not because they are all paedophiles or preferential child abusers, but simply because they are prostitute users in a place where large numbers of prostitutes are under the age of 18.

It is not only 'traditional' prostitute users who sexually exploit women, men and children in Goa. Sexual exploiters are also now drawn from the ranks of tourists and expatriates. The identities and the motivations of 'new' sexual exploiters are considered below.

New Sex Exploiters

In the 1960s and '70s, western hippies visited India in relatively large numbers. Three factors underpinned the influx of hippy tourists (many of whom went on to become expatriates):

- the extreme disparity of wealth between India and European countries (in the 1970s, there were British hippies who boasted that if they saved one month's dole money they could afford to travel to India on the 'Magic Bus' and live well for 6 months);
- the relatively safe, cheap and easy access to a range of drugs in India;
- an exoticising racist ideology which held India and the Indian people to be culturally 'Other'—more 'spiritual', more 'friendly', more 'accepting' than people of European and North America.

Goa received more than its fair share of such hippy tourists (indeed, Ajuna and Vagator in particular were home to what could virtually be described as colonies of expatriate hippies and their visiting friends), perhaps because as well as offering great natural beauty and miles of unspoilt beaches, its very recent history of Portugese colonial rule marked it out as somehow more 'European' than other parts of India.

The early western hippy 'settlers' helped to construct the conditions under which today's' drug tourism' developed, for Goa now finds itself host to large numbers of young westerners whose primary purpose in visiting the province is to attend 'acid parties' and raves and to consume drugs.

Older hippies and other foreigners, local Goans and migrants from Kashmir are involved in the organisation of these parties (which can attract as many as 1,500 people in high season—Barbosa, 1996) as well as in the drug trade.

Although it was not possible for us to systematically investigate the social identities of ageing hippies and drug tourists in Goa, our observational and interview work suggested to us that the older hippies who had spent many years in Goa (either on and off or as virtual expatriates) were either people from working class backgrounds who saw greater opportunities for 'wheeling and dealing' in India than they would have had back in Europe or North America, or else they were people who remained because they were suffering from serious psychological and/or drug related problems.

By contrast, a majority of the younger drug tourists appeared to be from middle class backgrounds.

The young westerners wandering around Anjuna flea market, for example, are decked out in 'radical chic' clothing and accessories that are extremely costly in Europe—their Rayban sunglasses, Nike footwear, personal stereos and cameras belie the carefully affected disregard for material wealth implied by their style of dress as well as the anarchistic slogans on their T-shirts.

They are status and image conscious people who flick through magazines like 'ID' and 'Loaded' as they sunbathe on the beach and they look forward to boasting to friends back home about having seen cult Goan diskjockeys such as 'Ohmegalpha' and 'Rock Trueman'.

These are young people with affluent parents and/or relatively large disposable incomes. Some of them are market traders who come to Goa to buy cheaply the kind of 'ethnic' gear they will sell for high prices back home.

All of them want sun and drugs and a taste of 'the exotic'. This means consuming the sight of other human beings' poverty and misery as though it were a form of entertainment or 'education' provided for their benefit.

These right-on young people pick their way between the brightly coloured stalls and the polio victims scrabbling through the dust, stopping to take photographs of littl beggar children on their way and exclaiming, 'Isn't it great It's just like Camden market!' Many of these young dru tourists travel as couples and we found no evidence t suggest that the single males among them were particularl interested in sexually exploiting local people (exploitin them economically was sufficient).

Those we interviewed said that they had never hear of prostitution in Goa. One of them had previously visite Thailand, where he had noticed both formal and inform prostitution, and had himself sexually exploited a youn Thai woman but he had not encountered anything simil during his month long stay in Goa. The fact that he wa quite open about his experiences in Thailand suggests h was reporting truthfully. This does not mean that youn male drug tourists never find their way to red light distric or sexually exploit women or children in Goa. No doubt ta driver/pimps offer to provide them with the same 'service that they offer other types of tourist and no doubt some them accept the offer.

However, it does seem that the cross-over between yout drug-tourism and sex-tourism is not especially pronounce so far as male tourists are concerned. Single female dru tourists are a different matter. Many of them do appear view sexual access to a local man as part and parcel of th 'experience' they consume on their 'exotic' holiday (fema sex-tourism is discussed in more detail below). But it doubtful that young western female drug-tourists a involved in the sexual exploitation of children. The san cannot be said of older male drug and hippy tourists ar expatriates as the following portrait, based on a lengt interview with one such man, shows.

Dave

Dave is a British man in his late forties. He was broug up in a tough, working class environment (in Brixton, Sou

London) and had a hard, miserable childhood. He started using drugs in his teens and was sectioned to a psychiatric hospital, where he spent several months at the age of 20. He first visited Goa in the 1970s and has returned many times since then, often staying for long periods.

When we met Dave he was drunk and drugged in a restaurant in a small Goan tourist town. He bore the bruises from a recent fight with some British package tourists and was extremely depressed.

But the story he told about his life and travels was a narrative about a man pitting himself against threats and dangers and triumphing over them. At the most basic level, his triumphs are economic and this makes them simultaneously triumphs over the British class system.

In Britain, a man from Dave's background can hope at best to support himself through factory or labouring work and those are exactly the type of jobs that he worked in his youth. In 'third world' countries by contrast, Dave has been able to make enough money to support himself and his travels in a variety of ways, none of which involve the daily humiliations and unfreedoms that are imposed on manual labourers in Britain.

Moreover, the ways in which he makes money in countries like India almost all involve 'fleecing' westerners who are more affluent, but less travelwise and more racist, than he. For instance, he told us that he had worked as a guide for tourists in the Himalayas.

On these treks, you know, through the mountains. They wanted a white guide, see, they don't trust 'natives', they think it's still Empire days. So I'd tell them I was a guide, knew the mountains like the back of me hand, give them a load of bullshit, take their money, then I'd pay a local to guide us and give them a lot more bullshit. They loved it.

He also makes money through drug dealing, organising small acid parties in Goa, arranging the sound systems for bigger parties, and disk-jockeying. Again, his financial success in such activities can be largely attributed to the fact that while tourists imagine his whiteness makes him more 'trustworthy' than an Indian or Kashmiri drug dealer or party organiser. And these activities have proved lucrative. Dave not only now owns his own home in Brixton but, on the evening we interviewed him, kept displaying a very large wad of dollar bills and also showed us a very expensive camcorder he had recently purchased.

His economic success testifies not just to the extent of white racism amongst tourists (who are clearly willing to pay hefty cuts to white middlemen in order to avoid direct dealings with 'natives') but also to Dave's very real triumph over his destiny. Of course, it is possible to make equally large sums of money as a 'wheeler-dealer' in Britain but it is a more high risk activity and his money goes a lot further in India.

Dave had visited red light districts in Thailand, Burma and Vietnam and had also been to a red light area in Bombay to look at the caged prostitutes. He said that he had simply gone to look and had never entered into a commercial sexual transaction in any of these places.

He described them with what seemed to be genuine disgust and horror and said he found child prostitution especially shocking. He said he had never been to a red light district in Goa and neither he, nor any of his companions, appeared to know where these districts are. All claimed never to have seen prostitution in Goa. It was something they only associated with Bombay, Delhi and Calcutta.

Although Dave did not define himself as a prostitute-user, he did describe entering into exploitative commercial transactions with Kamatakan children whilst in Goa.

For example, he had taken a fancy to the 16 years old sister of his Karnatakan masseur and had negotiated sexual access to her through her brother for a small sum of money. He had asked whether the girl, who was six months pregnant, would give him a 'special massage' for 300 rupees.

But, he hastened to assure us, this was not 'prostitution' since she was not a prostitute and he was not purchasing penetrative sex. 'She only gives me a blow job. That doesn't count'.

There is no reason to assume that Dave is alone in making such 'arrangements'. Older hippies, who either live in or frequently visit Goa, tend to rent private accommodation rather than staying in hotels or guest houses, and so enjoy the kind of privacy which facilitates this type of child abuse.

Although some live as virtually penniless 'bums', many of them make or have enough money to pay the small sums asked by relatives of young girls.

Hardened Sex Tourists, Paedophiles and Preferential Child Sex Abusers

There is reason to believe that a small number of men who might be described as 'hardened' sex tourists have identified Goa as a site in which they can cheaply accommodate their sexual interests.

We use the term 'hardened' sex tourist to refer to those western men who repeatedly travel to a variety of 'third world' countries where they know that commodified sex is extremely cheap and that a range of different sexual experiences will be available to them as 'consumers'.

Because, in their pursuit of 'experience', such men visit poverty stricken and seamy red light districts where large numbers of prostitutes are aged between 12 and 18, they are likely to sexually abuse children whether or not thev have a focussed sexual preference for children. We were not able to interview any such men in Goa but prostitutes working in the red light area we visited reported that western male tourists do, on occasion, buy their services.

Usually, such men take the woman or girl of their choice back to their hotel or apartment for the night, or even for a period of days, but it is not unknown for them to exploit the prostitute in her regular place of work.

There are also paedophiles and preferential child sex abusers who travel independently to Goa. Again, these men sometimes make use of red light districts where they know that their tastes will be catered to.

We spoke to a girl aged 11 who, along with a prostitute woman in her early 20s, had been taken by a tourist (she thought he was German) to a hotel in a tourist resort some miles distant from the red light area in which she lived.

This child worked in the bars as a dancer but, having not reached puberty, she was not yet prostituted. The tourist claimed that he wanted the child to accompany him and the older prostitute as their masseuse and he kept the two of them with him for eight days.

The girl said she had been provided with a separate room and that 'nothing had happened'. The tourist, she said, had 'only kissed and cuddled' her.

Other prepubertal girls have been taken away by tourists for several days at a time and when questioned by the nuns working in the district and/or other non-prostitute women, all provide this exact same response—'nothing happened', and when pressed further, 'he only kissed and cuddled me'.

It may be the case that all these little girls have been abused by paedophiles whose sexual interests are limited to non-genital touching and fondling. It seems more likely, however, that the girls are either discouraged from reporting the extent of their sexual abuse to authority figures by the pimps who have sold their bodies, or that they have no language to report it in or that it causes them shame and embarrassment to speak of what has happened to them in detail.

It is not necessary for preferential abusers and paedophiles to visit red light areas in order to obtain sexual access to children. They can and do approach beach seller children and make them direct offers, or they can obtain access to such children *via* an intermediary (in exactly the same way that Dave did).

If they are living in private accommodation rather than in hotels, then the whole process of child abuse—from negotiating access on—can be conducted in almost complete privacy. It is impossible to make even a meaningful guess at the scale of this type of abuse.

The only hard evidence to give any indication of the extent of the problem is the fact that, in 1995, the Department of Forensic Medicine at Bambolim 'received nearly 60 cases of sexually abused children, mostly pubescent boys from the tourist-heavy coastal areas' (Baria, 1996).

Since the number of children requiring medical attention as a result of sexual abuse is certainly far smaller than the number of children who are victims of sexual abuse, this is an even more alarming statistic than at first appears.

The interview we conducted with an expatriate Briton living in Goa and suspected of being a child sex abuser may provide some insight into the motivations of men who abuse in the informal prostitution sector.

We cannot state with absolute certainty that this man, Richard, is a practising abuser (although a British tabloid journalist claims to have evidence that he is and a number of local people are certain that he is sexually abusing children), but he closely conforms to the psychological profile of one type of paedophile, and his beliefs about Goa and attitudes towards Goans may therefore help to answer questions about why other paedophiles travel to Goa in order to practice their abuse.

Richard

Richard is from a middle class background (his father was the head teacher of a small private school) but he alludes to an unhappy childhood, saying that he was not 'brought up' by anyone at all. He was married but has no children of his own, and he is extraordinarily sentimental about his ex-wife. He describes his relationship with her as 'a Barbara Cartland story'.

In 1975 they divorced, and because he 'loved her so much' he made a fantastically generous financial settlement and, having 'ruined' himself, embarked upon a journey that would take him as far away as possible from his broken dreams:

I used to read Somerset Maugham, and I wanted to be like one of his characters. I wanted to be alone, surrounded by sun, sand and palm trees. I was thinking of the South Sea Islands. I wanted to get right away from everything. I thought of all the things I didn't need, car, television, newspapers, and I wanted to be where these things didn't even exist. I wanted to be somewhere way out of civilisation.

So, Richard bought a train ticket to Istanbul and set off. Once he arrived in Istanbul, he found himself surrounded by lots of young Germans who were 'slightly freaky, but well educated and intelligent'. They were trekking overland to India and Richard decided to go with them.

In describing his journey, Richard emphasises both the youth and vitality of his hippie companions and the 'dangers' he faced as he made his voyage into the 'uncivilised' world. Finally, he ended up in Goa where he spent four months swimming in the sea and hanging out on the beaches with young Europeans. At this point Richard's story degenerates into pure, and very revealing, narcissism:

I became healthy, and so brown, I was almost black. I was the darkest man on the beach. I was thin, I lost all my weight, I was thin and dark and handsome. I was so fit. People were amazed by how dark I was... I decided to stay... I went back to England to sort things out for a permanent move, and when I went into my old local, there were all my old friends, sitting in the same pub, almost as though they were sitting where I'd left them.

And they were all looking at me, they couldn't believe their eyes. I was so thin and dark and handsome, and they were all thinking 'How can I do the same thing?'

But they were trapped with mortgages and wives and children. I was free. He returned to Goa where, according to his narrative, he succeeded in everything he did—(whether that was running a restaurant, writing for a local paper or working as a tour representative for a package tour company) and he attracted yet more admiring gazes from everyone he came into contact with. He loved Goa. The people were so 'simple'.

That was what he liked so much, their 'simplicity'. He also found himself surrounded by children or, more particularly, young boys. Initially, these young local boys were fascinated by an old car he was doing up. 'Swarms' of young boys came to watch. He let them help. They enjoyed it. Now he is running his own travel agency business and is still surrounded by boys and young men.

For some twenty years then, Richard has found in Goa's 'Otherness' a mirror which reflects back an image of himself as the 'boy' he simultaneously desires and longs to be, and also an image of the 'fine, upstanding man' he considers himself to be.

In this sense, he is remarkably similar to abusive expatriates/regular visitors that we have interviewed in other sex tourist destinations. Back home, they feel themselves to be insignificant, overlooked, defeated, aging.

In the 'Third World', their money and their whiteness have restorative powers. But such men are also invariably ambivalent about the fantasy world over which they preside.

Richard, like other men of his kind, looks back to the halycon days of his first arrival and asserts that Goa is changing. Local Goan people were very tolerant and accepting of foreigners in the 1970s, he told us.

No one cared about the hippies or about nudism. 'You could do what you liked and no one gave a fig.' But now tourism has developed and the 'simplicity' of the Goan people is disappearing. According to Richard, 'They' are becoming more materialistic, more money conscious.

We asked him whether tourism was generating a growth in prostitution. He insisted there was no female prostitution worth mentioning in Goa but acknowledged that informal homosexual prostitution exists.

This, according to Richard, 'is very discreet and very understandable, because it's so difficult for young boys here to have relationships with girls. Sex is very much taboo outside marriage.' He pondered for a while on the problems that local young men face because of religious and cultural strictures against premarital sex, arguing that this explained their willingness to engage in sexual relationships with western men.

'It's very sad for them if they happen to fall in love with a tourist, though, because then they're so hurt when the man leaves'. But, he assured us, sexual relationships between boys and western men are not 'viewed in the same way here'. Does that mean it causes no psychological damage to the boys, we asked. 'No, probably not. And they benefit financially, you see,' he replied, 'so that makes a big difference to them'.

We have no firm evidence that Richard is an abuser but these three ideas (that teenage boys are 'deprived' of opportunities for heterosexual sex; that homosexual encounters are acceptable in this culture; and that boys benefit from such encounters) are precisely the kind of cognitive distortions employed by preferential child abusers in order to justify their own behaviour.

They give a clue as to how other western men who sexually exploit boys in Goa may rationalise their acts of abuse.

The idea that the boys have a biological sexual drive or 'natural curiosity' which is being stifled and that they are thus eager for sexual experimentation allows abusers to tell themselves that their victims actively *consent* to their sexual exploitation. (Sexual value is also attached to the boys' assumed heterosexuality by many men who either do not fully accept their own homosexual impulses or have a sexual interest in the 'corruption' of 'innocence'.)

The idea that the host culture is tolerant of teenage male homosexuality allows the abuser to assure himself that no psychological or social harm will come to the boy as a result of a sexual relationship with him. And finally, because the boys receive money and gifts, abusers can tell themselves that the children *benefit* from their abuse.

Male Homosexual Sex Tourists

As well as paedophiles and preferential child sex abusers, there are some western homosexual sex tourists who travel independently to Goa.

In general, westerners misread the social codes about physical contact between Indian men which allow male friends to hold hands, sit very close to each other, put arms around each other's shoulders etc., forms of contact which in the west are assumed to imply sexual intimacy.

Through many westerners' eyes, India appears to be a country which tolerates very open and public displays of sexual affection between men, and they therefore assume that homosexuality is acceptable within Indian society.

Nothing could be further from the truth, of course (India's homophobia is so great that homosexual acts between consenting adults are still illegal), and the social and economic consequences for boys and men who enter into sexual 'friendships' with male tourists can be serious.

Such truths would be inconvenient for those who wish to sexually exploit the economic misfortunes of 'Third World' peoples. It serves their interests better to tell themselves that 'prostitution is a way of life out here', or 'children grow up much quicker out here', or 'all the men are bisexual out here', and so on, *ad nauseum.*

Like heterosexual sex tourists, homosexual sex tourists who have no specific or focussed sexual interest in children may become 'situational' child abusers in the poor countries they visit. This is partly because homosexuals are as prone as heterosexuals to attach sexual value to youth and to be indifferent to the question of whether the boy they pursue is 15 or 25, so long as he is of a physical 'type' that they find attractive. It is also because those who are driven to informal prostitution are often under the age of 18, and because the ideas and stereotypes discussed above serve to reduce the sex tourist's inhibitions around sexually exploiting minors. The information for gay travellers provided in the *Rough Guide to India* (a guide book popular in the English speaking world) is worth noting here.

The guide observes that western interpretations of physical contact between men are often incorrect, but then continues: On the other hand, as in many countries where heterosexual contact outside of marriage is difficult, homosexual behaviour is frequent among people who do not consider themselves gay, and a surprising number of Indian men are bisexual. For this reason, one-offs are more likely than long-term relationships (Abram *et al.*, 1995: 64).

It is no doubt the case that there are many gay and bisexual men in India but questions about the extent of homosexuality amongst Indian men are irrelevant to a discussion of sex tourism. What the *Rough Guide* fails to point out is that the gay traveller is far more likely to come in contact with, and secure sexual access to, Indian males who are far from their equals in terms of economic power and often a great deal younger than them, than they are to come in contact with mature, affluent bisexual or gay men. The likelihood of a sexual encounter which takes place across massive inequalities in terms of economic power and age being underpinned by genuine consent and reciprocal desire is slim.

Because most sex tourists (heterosexual, homosexual and paedophile) would prefer to explain local people's apparent willingness to have sex with them through reference to 'cultural' factors (and/or their own personal charm) than to recognise that this 'willingness' is based simply in economic desperation, the *Rough Guide's* comments will inevitably be interpreted by sex tourists as a tailor-made justification for the serial sexual exploitation of local men and boys.

Female Sex Tourists

If a sex tourist is defined as a tourist who enters into sexually exploitative relationships with local, women, children and/or men whilst on holiday, then it is possible to describe some women as sex tourists. In Goa, as in other 'Third World' holiday destinations, it is possible to observe female tourists who use their greater economic power in such locations in order to indulge racialised sexual fantasies with local men or boys. In Goa, aside from the domestic tourists discussed below, western women are the most visible group of sex tourists. India as a whole attracts relatively large numbers of single western female tourists /travellers, and this, is also the case in Goa, where the gender composition of the western tourist body is noticeably skewed towards women.

Not *every* single female tourist enters into sexual relationships with Indian men whilst on holiday. And of those who do not all can be described as engaging in a sexually exploitative relationship. Some enter into sexual relationships with men who are the same age as themselves or older and who are their economic equals.

We spoke to a number of successful Kashmiri entrepreneurs, for example, who either had, or had in the past, formed sexual relationships with western tourist women of their own age or younger.

Such relationships are probably best characterised as mutually casual (neither side was interested in marriage or long-term commitment), and mutually objectifying (each party seemed to be equally motivated by a set of 'exoticising'-racist assumptions about the other).

On the whole, however, there is an imbalance, often a massive imbalance, between these women and their sexual partners in terms of their economic power and there is also often an imbalance in terms of their ages. We observed women in their fifties with men in their late teens/early twenties, for example.

The distorting powers of racist, sexist and sexual/moral ideologies should not be overlooked, and it may well be that in some cases, the men/boys concerned would pursue sexual relationships with 'available' western women even if there was no economic incentive for so doing. Certainly, this is what western women like to tell themselves. Those we interviewed (and this is true of those who had not formed sexual relationships with local men, as well as those who had) tended to hold a view of local men as sexually predatory and to describe themselves and other western women as the victims of unwanted attentions from Indian men.

In particular, they would remark on the behaviour of domestic Indian sex tourists, saying how 'sick and tired' they were of being oggled, propositioned and photographed on the beach. But whether or not the men/boys who enter into sexual relationships with them are driven by sexual/ sexualised racial fantasies or by straightforward economic considerations, the fact remains that western women are usually so economically powerful in relation to them that their interaction inevitably takes on some of the character of prostitution.

The women invariably pay for meals, drinks and entertainment and they buy their 'lovers' clothing, footwear and other gifts. In return, the men provide flattering sexual and other attentions as well as acting as guides and companions. The women's greater economic power also furnishes them with a great deal of control within the relationship. They decide when, where and what to eat; where to go and what to do each day, and so on.

These may seem like small details, but they very clearly reverse both western and Indian gender norms, and it is disingenuous for western women to claim that they are 'unaware' of the unaccustomed power they wield within such relationships.

In principal, we see no moral grounds for objecting to sexual liaisons between adults which take place on the basis of informed consent and where neither party has been coerced into the liaison, either by another person or by economic necessity. But it is worth noting that in Goa, even relationships which meet these moral criteria can have harmful consequences if, for example, the man concerned is already married.

The following story told to us by one informant illustrates the way in which, despite indulging in apparently consensual and non-exploitative relationships, western women tourists can be a highly destructive force in local people's lives.

Sheela is a girl from Karnataka who lives in Goa. At the age of seven she was married to her uncle, then aged 18. Her husband is now 24 years old and pursues sexual relationships with western women tourists.

He does not do this in order to support himself or his family, but the material advantages he pursues through his relationships with western women are none the less real and compelling ones.

These women hold out to him the promise of the kind of lifestyle and possessions that confer status (fashionable western clothing, riding rented motorbikes, eating in good restaurants, drinking expensive drinks, etc.), and there is always the possibility of the gift of a handsome sum of money, enough to set up a business, buy property, transform his life in some way.

When he is 'successful' in picking up a tourist, he spends as much time as he can in her company, staying with her overnight, eating with her and generally disregarding the expectations of his wife and family.

Although only 13 years old, Sheela faces a choice between divorcing her husband, an act which would effectively condemn her to social death, or living with constant humiliation and insecurity.

Macho Lads

Goa is now experiencing mass 'budget' tourism, brought to the state by European package operators who, since the late 1980s, have sought to exploit it as a profit opportunity.

The extent and speed of the growth of package tourism is illustrated by the fact that where in 1985-86 only 3,568 tourists arrived on charter flights, by 1994-95, their number had risen to 59,881 (de Souza, 1995). On the whole, these package tourists are couples, pensioners and young people in search of cheap sun, sea, sand (and often drugs). At present, the vast majority of package tourists have absolutely no interest in sexually exploiting local people whilst on holiday (indeed, many would prefer to have as little to do with local people as possible while in Goa).

However, the growth of package tours to the region does make sex tourism a great deal cheaper for all the different types of sexual exploiter described above. Excess seats on charter flights from Britain to Goa sell for as little as £ 120 and last minute deals on packages drop as low as £ 300 for a two week vacation.

The extraordinarily low cost of package holidays to Goa also means that they are well within reach of single, unskilled British manual workers; in fact, even unemployed Britons can afford a holiday in this 'tropical paradise'. Because a working class male subculture of 'Macho Lad' sex tourists has now developed in western European societies (see O'Connell Davidson, 1995, and O'Connell Davidson and Sanchez Taylor, 1996), any 'Third World' holiday destination which provides cheap and easy sexual access to prostitute women and children risks becoming the focus of mass sex tourism.

Goa already attracting a small number of this type of tourist. On the charter flight on which we travelled we interviewed four men, two of whom were in their late twenties, two in their early thirties. They were travelling together and had bought a two week package deal for £ 320 each.

Two were in unskilled manual occupations, two were unemployed, but occasionally did casual work. Their only previous experience of foreign travel was a trip that the four of them had taken together to Amsterdam, the primary purpose of which was to smoke marijuana and use prostitutes.

When asked why they had chosen to take a holiday in Goa, one replied, 'Because it's cheap.' Another said. 'We've heard that prostitutes are 20p [£ 0.2 sterling] a go out there.' They had a friend who had been on a package holiday to Goa the year before and 'he said it was great. Really cheap out there'.

We asked whether they would use prostitutes given the opportunity. One said no. The others answered that they would. 'Yes. If a girl came up and she was pretty. Why not? For a quid,' one said.

Later, one of the Macho Lads who had said he would use prostitutes if they were available, began to complain about the bureaucratic procedure it is necessary to go through to get a visa for a holiday in Goa. 'I had to queue for ages; he said, 'and it was all Pakkies in there. The whole place was full of Pakkies'. We asked him whether he had any Asian friends or acquaintances in Britain. 'No,' he told us. 'I don't like them. They keep themselves to themselves anyway'. Why, if he did not like 'Them', we wondered, was he interested in the idea of using a prostitute in Goa? Was be attracted to Indian women?

No, they're horrible. Well, you never see them, do you? They don't go out. You don't see them in the pub or anything like that. Anyway, they're dirty. I used to work as a postman, so I've seen.

It was hard to tell whether he grasped the significance of the question, however, since he not only expressed surprise at the fact that there were Indian people at the Indian Consulate where he had gone to get his visa but also appeared to have no idea that he was actually going to India.

On the plane, he picked up an in-flight magazine with a map of flight routes and asked us to point out where Goa was. He was looking at the page which mapped flights around Europe. Taxi driver/pimps play a pivotal role in facilitating sex tourism for this type of sex tourist. This man, for example, who cannot even locate Goa on a map and who 'hates Pakkies' would hardly be able to independently research the existence of red light areas, make his way to them and negotiate access to a prostitute woman or child.

Two other Macho Lads we interviewed confirmed the importance of third party involvement. Jack and Alan had arrived together on a package tour and it was Jack's second visit to Goa. On his first trip, a taxi driver had taken him to a red light district where he had used a prostitute. Jack therefore took it upon himself to introduce Alan to the delights of sexual exploitation.

Again, without having been introduced to the area and reassured as to the safety of foreign men in that area by the taxi driver, it seems unlikely that Jack would have practised sex tourism in Goa, and he would not therefore have been in a position to encourage other 'lads' to do likewise.

Domestic Sex Tourists

Angle (1994:9) observes that within a few years of liberation, Goa started being projected as the 'Rome of the

East', 'a westernised society,' 'a predominantly Catholic state having a culture markedly different from that of the rest of the country'.

The Portugese legacy of an annual carnival, along with different dress codes for women, for instance, were viewed by non-Goan Indians as a mark of westernisation. The presence of significant numbers of western hippies in the state from the mid-60s onwards further enhanced this image of Goa as 'different' from the rest of India, especially since the behaviour and lifestyle of the hippies was so wildly at odds with the values and mores of their host society.

Although, such people fondly imagined themselves to be sensitive to the culture and religions of local people, nothing could have been further from the truth. In particular, their drug use was and remains a crime, and their style of dress and practice of nudism on beaches was and remains extraordinary and offensive to most Goan people.

The growing number of western women tourists sunbathing topless and forming casual sexual relationships with local men further 'sexualised' Goa, reinforcing the general stereotype non-Goan Indians held of Goa as a westernised and liberal state.

Around 80 per cent of Goa's tourism is domestic. Many of these Indian tourists arrive in family groups or travel with their spouse and are drawn to Goa by its natural beauty, climate, and so on. But there is reason to believe that the stereotypes about Goa mentioned above have also fuelled a form of domestic sex tourism. The gender composition of domestic tourists is skewed toward men and the primary 'leisure' activities of many domestic male tourists are sexual.

They 'oggle' western women on the beaches, often asking them to pose for photographs or taking photos of them topless without asking their permission. They also visit red light districts by the bus load, where they drink in bars, watch the 'dancing girls' and buy sexual access to prostituted women and children.

In Thailand, gangs of young British, Garman and Swedish 'Macho Lads' are to be seen strutting along beaches and through the red light areas, and in the Caribbean and Latin America, groups of Italian and Spanish 'Lads' behave in similar ways, but in Goa, it is gangs of young male Indian tourists who swagger the beaches and red light districts.

Older men from various regions of India are also to be seen in the red light areas and prostitutes working in these districts report that a good deal of their custom comes from domestic tourists to Goa.

Because large numbers of prostitutes working in Goa's red light districts are under the age of 18, men who buy sexual services are likely to become child sex abusers whether or not they have a focussed sexual interest in children.

It is probably the case that in numerical terms domestic sex tourists in Goa represent the single largest group of child sex exploiters. It is equally likely to be the case that very few of them would be clinically diagnosable as 'paedophiles' or 'hebephiles'. They become child abusers simply because they are prostitute-users in a setting where no one appears to care much about the fact that girls as young as 12 years of age are prostituted for commercial gain and/or their own subsistence.

TOURISM AND CHILD SEXUAL EXPLOITATION IN GOA: THE RISK OF WESTERN EXPANSION

It is virtually impossible to provide accurate figures on the numbers of foreign sex tourists visiting any given location. We can only make 'best guesses' based on assessments of certain key 'indicators'.

For example, we can look at a resort like Pattaya, Thailand, which attracts around 1.5 million foreign visitors annually, consider statistics which show that the gender composition of tourist arrivals in Thailand is around 75% male (Truong, 1990), observe that 'entertainment' provided for tourists in Pattaya revolves solely around the sex industry and that virtually all tourists in Pattaya are male, and estimate that somewhere between 80 and 90 per cent of those 1.5 million foreign visitors are sex exploiters.

On the basis of the same type of reasoning, we would say that while there is a problem of tourist sexual exploitation in Goa, the state has certainly seen nothing yet so far as mass western sex tourism goes.

Given that mass western sex tourism can develop very rapidly (consider, for instance, the case of Cuba), it is important to examine the factors which are likely to promote or discourage this form of development in Goa.

Comparing Goa against other sites of sex tourism usefully highlights such factors.

Comparing Sex Tourist Destinations: The Familiar and the Unfamiliar 'Exotic'

As yet, Goa's informal prostitution sector has a very different character from that which exists in well established sites of sex tourism in other countries such as the Dominican Republic, Cuba or Brazil. The infrastructure of bars, discos, casinos and clubs which supports this type of prostitution elsewhere is not in place in Goa.

Street scenes at night in Goan resort towns are very different from those found in, say, Boca Chica where hoardes of drunken sex tourists throng in and out of bars and discos arm in arm with young Dominicans, engaging in mindless revelry until the early hours of the morning. In a town like

Calangute or Candolim, it is difficult to even get a drink after 10 p.m.

Another very striking difference is that females who are sexually exploited within this sector are controlled by a third party rather than soliciting autonomously. They are not usually in a position to enter into the kind of diffuse (and generally more remunerative) transactions entered into by their male counterparts.

The mass of sex tourists in other parts of the world are heterosexual men who want to pretend that the prostitutes they exploit are 'like girlfriends'. Although, some of our Goan informants felt that it would be possible for western men to openly parade Indian 'girlfriends' in the same way that western women parade their Indian 'boyfriends', in eight days of field- work we did not observe a single western man with an Indian woman/girl.

This almost certainly serves to inhibit the expansion of western sex tourism, for homosexual and female sex tourists are in a minority.

It might be objected that the informal beach based prostitution discussed above does provide sexual access to women and girls but we would argue that, as currently organised, Goa's beach prostitution would hold only limited appeal to 'ordinary' western sex tourists of the Mr. Average and Macho Lad type (see O'Connell Davidson, 1995).

Comparing beach prostitution in Thailand and Goa helps to explain this. In Thailand, freelance beach prostitutes dress in westernized clothing (and clothing that is considered 'sexy' in the west—microscopic bikinis, short skirts and crop tops, etc.). Part of their allure for western sex tourists is that they are 'different' from western women but not too different.

Most Thai sex workers are also skilled professionals with a sales patter (the basic line is 'You're a sexy man', 'Do you like me?', 'You want fucky fucky?', which is elaborated upon according to the woman's language and thespian skills). Again, this script is familiar to western men.

In Thailand, the western sex tourist finds himself surrounded by the 'exotic' (palm trees, white sands, 'beautiful' dark skinned, glossy haired girls) *and* by the familiar (the 'beautiful' girls dress and behave exactly as western girls do, but are a great deal more flattering and cheaper).

In Goa, by contrast, beach prostitution is not marked in ways that are familiar to westerners or easy for them to decipher. The Karnatakan and Rajasthani women and girls who walk the beach in full traditional costume selling lungis, jewellery and massage are not instantly identifiable to westerners as sexually available (indeed, many of them are not) or even sexually interesting.

It was also our strong impression that even those women and children who are sometimes prostituted to foreign men do not self-identify as sex workers and so would not have developed the kind of sales patter used by Thai sex workers.

To independently negotiate sexual access to such women/ girls would require foreign men to decode quite subtle and culturally variable 'clues', and it seems highly unlikely to us that the kind of Macho Lads and Mr. Averages we have interviewed in other sex tourist destinations would have either the confidence or the ability to do this. They would therefore need a third party, such as a pimp, to make the availability of sexual services explicit. Such third parties are involved in beach prostitution and there are also third parties who offer to arrange visits to red light districts or to bring prostitutes to hotel rooms.

Although there are, without doubt, western package tourists who take pimps up on these offers, it is important to recognise that this dependence on third party involvement makes Goa differ from other popular sex tourist resorts in ways that western sex tourists would not necessarily like.

To begin with, it makes prostitution far more explicit and the tourist's role in it thus becomes transparent.

One significant difference between prostitute use back home and prostitute use in most sex tourist destinations is that whereas in their own countries men have to make a conscious decision to seek out and use prostitutes, in a resort like Pattaya or Sosua they can tell themselves that their prostitute use 'just happened'.

Even though many western sex tourists do make very explicit decisions to visit brothels, strip shows and live sex shows, for the majority of these men, such visits punctuate, rather than structure, their orgy of sexual indulgence abroad. In between purchasing highly commodified forms of sex, they like to pick up freelance and bar-based prostitutes and tell themselves that these are 'nice girls' who are 'not like real prostitutes.'

They construct their transactions with such 'girls' as something different from the short time transactions they enter into in brothels, and they like to believe that they were *chosen* by the girl in question (a beautiful young girl approached them and offered herself and what could they do but accept?) and not that *they* have arranged access to her through an intermediary.

For a man to be approached and feel himself chosen and wanted in this way in Goa, he would have to go and hang out in a bar in a red light district and, at present, a number of things militate against large numbers of western sex tourists doing this. The red light districts are not integrated into the resorts used by western package tour operators as they are elsewhere in the world. It is cheap enough for a man to get a taxi to them but it seems to as unlikely that 'ordinary' western sex tourists would be happy to get out of the taxi and wander around such districts, even in groups.

Unlike western sailors and experienced 'travellers', many of these men would be extremely unnerved and threatened to find themselves the sole white presence in a district full of Indians. This is especially true of 'first time' visitors, such as the four Macho Lads described above, who 'hate Pakkies' and are even disconcerted by the presence of Indians in an Indian consulate. Even sex tourists who are slightly more experienced will not necessarily feel good about visiting such districts because, unlike red light areas in popular sex tourist destinations, they share few features with western red light districts. In Thailand, the red light areas of Pattaya and Patpong are lined with western style ago-go bars, western pop music blares out of them and girls in western style 'sexy' outfits dance western style within them.

In Goa, the bars in the red light areas are mainly small, dingy and dirty, the music is unfamiliar to the western ear and the girls perform a Hindi dance to it. The style of dress adopted by prostitute women is very modest by western standards. Indeed, apart from the odd prostitute who is doing well and can afford to wear jeans, high heels and blouses, the majority appear to the western eye to be wearing traditional costumes.

It seems to us that this kind of unfamiliarity would be experienced as disconcerting by the kind of western sex tourists who are found in large numbers elsewhere in the world. In our view, the reaction of one man (who had happily practised sex tourism in Keyna and the Dominican Republic) to a Goan red light area, would not be an uncommon one:

It was terrible. I was really shocked. It was disgusting. There were young boys, only about nine or ten years old, sitting outside in the dirt with these older blokes, you know, selling them.

And it stank, it was disgusting, just the thought of what was inside those places, I wouldn't go in, it was disgusting.

Clearly, some western sex tourists' sensibilities are not even this developed (for example, Jack, mentioned earlier, had used a prostitute in a Goan red light area) but we would still argue that the very extreme unfamiliarity and 'Otherness' of Goa's red light districts militates against mass demand from western sex tourists.

None of this means that Goa is free from the threat of mass western sex tourism, however. Western sex tourism develops as stories of 'sexploits' are traded between 'blokes' in pubs and bars back home and recounted in smutty tabloid papers, soft porn magazines and over the Internet.

In this way, sex tourists multiply. They hear that 'prostitutes are 20p a go' somewhere and decide to have a look for themselves. Meanwhile, economic self-interest encourages sex workers, pimps and bar owners to learn how best to tap into new 'markets', and it is therefore to be expected that the trickle of western sex tourists who are (with the help of taxi driver/pimps) increasingly finding their way to red light districts, are teaching those who work in the sex industry a great deal about western tastes in commercial sexual transactions.

It would only take one or two enterprising souls to adjust the way in which commodified sex is packaged and presented, for others to recognise the enormous commercial potential of western sex tourism. Certainly, prostitutes working in red light districts (as well as beach seller children) are already aware that white men are willing and able to pay a lot more for sexual access than are migrant workers or locals. This provides a real incentive to learn the patter that pleases such men.

We were told one story about a shack owner turning his beach bar in a tourist area into the kind of take-out bar-brothel that appeals to western sex tourists (western pop music, girls in western dress, etc.). The story was unsubstantiated but this is essentially all that it would take for western sex tourists to find Goa a more attractive proposition.

The Role of Sexism, Racism and Indifference

Sex tourism is very clearly an expression of massive and obscene economic inequalities between affluent and poor countries, as well as between affluent individuals in poor countries and the mass of poor people. What is perhaps less immediately obvious is the way in which sex tourism rests on the articulation of a variety of sexisms and racisms and, above all, on peoples' seemingly endless capacity for indifference to the suffering of their fellow human beings.

Sex tourism in Goa is no exception to all this. Westerners' desire for sexual contact with local adults and children is often structured by their racist constructions of the exotic and erotic 'primitive,' while their racist assumptions about cultural 'difference' are used to justify and defend their sexually exploitative acts.

Sadly, it appears that domestic Indian tourists and local men are equally capable of 'Otherising' prostituted women and children through reference to assumed cultural, ethnic or caste 'differences'. Meanwhile, it seems that for some Goan people, the fact that the majority of prostituted women and children are migrants, and so 'Other', makes their fate a matter of indifference.

Just as the mass of sex tourists (western and Indian) employ sexist and misogynous ideas to demarcate good/bad women, madonnas/whores, women worthy of care and respect/degraded and worthless women, in order to justify sexually abusing them, so public indifference to the plight of prostituted girl children and women (which is rooted in the same sexist and misogynous ideas so dear to sex tourists) allows sex tourism to thrive.

It is often the case that the abuse of male children by paedophiles arouses a great deal of public indignation, while an equivalent degree of outrage and concern about far higher levels of abuse against girl children (especially those who are prostituted in red light districts) is noticeably absent.

Certainly those who are concerned about the expansion of sex tourism in Goa need to take the situation in the state's red light areas very seriously. As noted above, it is estimated that 1,000 children are at risk of sexual exploitation in one of these areas alone. These districts already cater to substantial numbers of heterosexual domestic sex tourists.

Demand from heterosexual western tourists has even greater commercial potential and this must already be clear to those who own and control 'business' in these areas. The way forward for truly entrepreneurial pimps, brothel and bar owners is obvious. But campaigns to drive prostituted women and children from these districts are *not* a solution. Where prostitution is the only means of subsistence for large numbers of people, harassing prostitutes only forces them to move to other (often more dangerous) areas and promotes the development of more highly organised forms of prostitution, controlled by people with the economic power to bribe police and officials.

At an international level, the poverty which underpins red light district prostitution and beach prostitution in Goa needs to be urgently addressed. For as things stand, one of the most depressing conclusions we came to during the course of our fieldtrip is that an influx of western sex tourists is probably the best hope that the majority of prostituted children in Goa have of raising their standard of living.

If this is so, it is perhaps *the* most bitter indictment imaginable of the affluent world's indifference to the suffering of children in poor countries.

BRITISH SEX TOURISTS IN THAILAND

I just get turned on very much by Orientals.... They're completely different... You... take a girl from a bar, and it might be eleven or twelve at night, and you have a shower and get in bed and have sex, and then most guys go sleep till next morning. Then they'll have a bit more in the morning and then she'll go. I've had them in the morning tidy up the room, fold me clothes up, even wash me socks, stuff like that. I was quite amazed to see it. I think they might've been after an extra tip on top....

You should never fall in love, or you'll be heartbroken when you leave. They might be heartbroken too. Because quite a few of them have got cuts on their arms here. They cut themselves with a knife. They get drunk and just slash themselves. I find that terrible. When I see a girl, when I'm looking to buy her, I always look at her arms to see what she's been doing to herself.

The term 'sex tourism' is widely associated with organised sex tours, often conjuring up images of groups of middle aged businessmen being shepherded into state sanctioned brothels in South Korea or ago-go bars in the Philippines and Thailand. But if sex tourism is defined as consisting of people from economically developed nations travelling to underdeveloped countries 'specifically to purchase the sexual services of local women [and men]' (Enloe, 1989:36), it embraces a far broader range of people, activities and locations.

Male sex tourists of all ages travel to Brazil and some African and Caribbean countries as well as to South East Asia. Bali, the Gambia and the Caribbean are popular destinations for female sex tourists. The nature and terms of the exchanges between sex tourists and local people vary enormously, as does the degree to which any third party, including the state, is involved.

A number of authors have discussed the economic, social, political, institutional and ideological factors which underpin the growth of sex tourism in South East Asia (Barry, 1979, 1984; Mitter, 1986; Heyzer, 1986; Enloe, 1989; Lee, 1991). This paper does not set out to contribute to debate in this area but will merely refer the reader to Truong's (1990) detailed and scholarly analysis of the phenomenon.

Instead, the primary aim of the paper is to provide some empirical data on the attitudes, motivations and activities of male British sex tourists in Thailand. For between 1980 and 1986, Britain supplied over a million of the 15.8 million tourists who visited Thailand, 73 per cednt of whom were male (Truong, 1990: 173-4) and it is important to ask what kind of people the hundred thousand or so British men who annually visit are, and why so many of them are prepared to travel so far in order to pay for sex.

Preliminary data from an on-going piece of research suggests that British sex tourists are not an entirely homogeneous group; they can be subdivided into three broad types, but for all these men, sex tourism in Thailand has three main attractions which, to varying degrees, shape their decision to travel for sex. The paper begins by developing a typology of sex tourists, then goes on to look at what they get out of sex tourism.

VARIETIES OF SEX TOURISTS

Of the British tourists I interviewed and observed who had chosen Thailand as a holiday destination specifically for sexual purposes, one clearly identifiable sub-group was made up of 'Macho Lads'. These men were typically skilled, semi- and unskilled manual workers in their early twenties. Not all are package tourists. In fact, those that I interviewed had all made their own travel arrangements. For most, this was at least their second or third visit to Pattaya (Thailand's premier sex resort) and all had first travelled to Thailand on the personal recommendation of another sex tourist. Macho Lads often travel in groups of three or four and those who arrive alone seem to quickly team up with others with whom they sunbathe, drink and visit clubs.

For these young men, Pattaya is a kind of macho theme park with beer, motorbikes, ago-go bars, kick boxing, live sex shows, pool tables in English style pubs and guaranteed access to dolly birds to posture with and have sex. Most of the Macho Lads interviewed said that they use prostitutes in England either regularly or occasionally, though some claimed never to have purchased sexual services anywhere except in Thailand.

As well as the Macho Lads, there are large numbers of men to whom I shall refer as 'Mr. Average'. Though most of these men were on second or third trips to Thailand, all of those I spoke to had originally come to Pattaya on package tours, some specifically targeted at 'single men'. Mr. Average is usually, but not always, older than the Macho Lad, and he is often divorced or widowed. He may be a skilled manual worker, self-employed or in a junior or middle management position, but he prides himself on being a respectable 'ordinary bloke'. He is primarily (though not exclusively) interested in simulating some kind of emotional or romantic relationship with either one woman or a series of women, rather than pursuing large numbers of anonymous sexual encounters.

These men describe Pattaya as 'Fantasy Island' and, except for the early evening period when they tend to sit round the hotel bar engaging in manly conversation with each other, they have a Thai woman on their arm at all times. Most claim never to visit prostitutes in Britain and do not consider themselves as clients even in Thailand.

Many people would, no doubt, explain the behaviour of Mr. Average and the Macho Lads through reference to their class position and their lack of formal education. But more bourgeois men also practice sex tourism. Numerous

'Cosmopolitan Men', well off, well read and well traveled, also buy sexual services in Thailand.

These men are keen to differentiate themselves from their compatriots 'I'm not a sex tourist', 'I'm not a package tourist', 'I am spending a few months travelling South East Asia', and 'I'm here on business really'. They visit more remote and less developed spots, they spend more time in Bangkok, but they also go to Patty for a few days in order to 'relax'. They are worldly-wise but they do not see themselves as the kind of men who frequent prostitutes. Several said that they would never use a prostitute anywhere else in the world.

In short, then, sex tourists do not constitute an entirely homogeneous group. They vary in terms of age and social class, and there are differences in terms of their willingness to see themselves as sex abusers. However, to a greater or lesser degree, all the three types described above are drawn to Thailand as sex tourists for three sets of reasons. *First*, commodity sex is cheap in Thailand and the degree of 'consumer' choice is immense.

Second, the nature and terms of exchange between prostitute and client in Thailand is very different from that between prostitute and client in Britain or any other European country. In Thailand the exchange is far less contractual and this makes it much more attractive to British men for a number of reasons. *Finally*, all three types of men find sex tourism affirmative of a particular 'radicalised' and sexualised masculine identity. The following sections discuss these issues in detail.

PRICE ADVANTAGES AND SOVEREIGN CONSUMERS

Any analysis of sex tourism which fails to consider its economics is doomed to provide only a partial explanation of the phenomenon, for without the obscene disparity in average per capita incomes between the countries which host sex tourists and those which supply them, sex tourism would be a marginal activity of a very different character. Feminists, socialists and policy makers may not all be entirely happy about the tourists who visit Amsterdam in order to buy sexual services from local people, for example, but because the power relations and economics involved here are of a very different order from those involved in sex tourism in underdeveloped countries, it does not excite the same moral and political repugnance.

Throughout the following discussion it must be borne in mind that whatever the complexity of British men's motivations, the bottom *line* in terms of explaining why they are in Thailand is cost. In Thailand, a prostitute can be rented for almost 24 hours for as little as 500 Baht (around £18), a sum of money that would barely secure a man a ten minute 'blow job' in Britain. The cheapness of sexual services (as well as of accommodation, food, drinks, travel and other services) furnishes a single, working class British man with a level of economic power that he could never enjoy at home or in any other European country, and all the sex tourists I interviewed commented on the fact that in Thailand they 'live like kings' or 'playboys'.

These men find themselves not only with untold economic power, they also find themselves 'spoilt for choice'. For in Thailand, the relationship between the tourist and the sex industry is so complex and multifaceted that the array of different forms of commoditised sex on offer to tourists is quite staggering. Truong (1990: 199) explains that the historical roots of this diversity lie in the fact that:

> The legal persecution of prostitutes occurred almost simultaneously with the legal formalisation of the entertainment industry, owing to an investment policy skewed towards capturing the Rest and Recreation market during the Indo-China conflict.

The duality between the recognition and denial of prostitution, coupled with a massive arrival of US military servicemen, led to a proliferation of forms of prostitution disguised within the entertainment industry. *Ad hoc* practices of hosting prostitution gradually became systemic as a result of the high rate of capital accumulation. (Truong 1990: 199).

Today this proliferation means that female, male and trans-sexual prostitutes are to be found working from a huge variety of settings—including brothels, bars, massage parlours, escort agencies, discos, hotels, streets, beaches. A range of more diffusely sexualised entertainment and personal services are also widely available in Bangkok and most major Thai resorts for example, cabarets which are mildly erotic rather than overtly sexual, beachside masseuses who caress feet, hands and backs but provide no direct genital stimulation.

Moreover, there is both a formal market for mail order brides and marriage bureaux catering almost exclusively to western men and an informal market consisting of women who independently seek western men for long term relationships, so that, in essence, tourists are provided with a continuum of opportunities to purchase sexual pleasure and rights of sexual access in Thailand. This continuum runs through from the mere pleasure of looking at sexually available women (and men and children) at one pole to the satisfaction of complete sexual possession at the other.

Thailand's sex industry has become a tourist attraction in itself and reputable guide books recommend a visit to red light districts (see Kusy, 1992). In these areas, tourists (even those who never go on to become sex-abusers) are provided with opportunities for voyeurism and mild titillation, pleasures which are generally paid for indirectly through the inflated prices of drinks, or directly through a cover charge made upon entering or leaving bars or live sex shows. For those tourists who do go on to purchase the services of a prostitute, the extent and visibility of 'vice' in these areas doubtless enhances their pleasure, for as Hoigard and Finstad (1986: 88) found in their study based in Oslo, 'some men find sexual value in peeping as a prelude to the act of prostitution'.

For tourists who want more than titillation, it is possible to purchase what is known as 'short time' with a prostitute. This service is generally on offer in massage parlours as well as at the ago-go and live sex show bars/brothels mentioned above. The tourist pays the parlour or bar owner a fee, which varies between 300 and 1,000 Baht £ 10-£ 25 then takes the prostitute of his choice to an upstairs room where he enjoys one or two hours of sexual access to her. A variation on this arrangement is found in bars which make a cover charge of around 500 Baht in exchange for which the customer receives one drink and the sexual attentions of a woman as they consume it. In Pattaya, for example, there is a bar known as the 'No Hands Bar' where prostitutes crawl under the tables in order to fellate the customers.

Men can also rent bar prostitutes for around 24 hours at a time. The client pays what is known as a 'bar fine' of 200 to 500 Baht to the bar plus a sum that is negotiated with the prostitute directly to her. Having paid the fine, the man is free to take the prostitute back to his hotel room for the whole night and most of the following day. The formal rationale for this is as follows. Bar owners employ people to work the bar (selling drinks, deaning up, chatting to customers) or as dancers. If a customer wants to take one of the workers away from the bar for the night, he must pay the bar owner a 'fine' in compensation for the loss of that person's labour.

In reality, however, these workers are rarely paid a regular wage by the bar owner, and there are always far more women or men attached to any one bar than is necessary to run it, so that the 'fine' system is actually a source of income for the bar owner who is effectively operating a 'take away' brothel. He gets his cut without having to support the overheads associated with providing rooms and facilities for clients who use their own hotel rooms.

Overnight deals can also be negotiated with freelance prostitutes who solicit outside bars and discos as well as from a variety of other settings, and it is worth noting that these 24 hour deals underline the extent to which the tourism and the sex industries are interwoven. Such arrangements would be impossible without the active collusion of hoteliers. Some hotels charge customers a fee for bringing a prostitute back for the night, others simply profit by the extra drinks and breakfasts sold and the custom won through not making a charge.

Many western package tour operators negotiate with hoteliers over these fees, for their absence is a major selling point; indeed, seasoned sex tourists state that this is the one real advantage of buying a package holiday rather than travelling independently.

Sex tourists can also enter into transactions of more extended duration with prostitutes, keeping the same woman with them for several days or weeks. This kind of arrangement is generally made with bar or freelance prostitutes following a 24 hour deal which has proved satisfactory to the sex client but can also sometimes be made with women who do not work full time as prostitutes. For those white men who want more than just this kind of 'long haul' deal, there is often the option of complete sexual possession through marriage. This can be arranged through one of the many agencies operating in Bangkok, or informally with the woman and/or her relatives.

Thailand thus offers an abundance of choice and diversity in terms of the sexual pleasures that can be bought and the kind of transactions involved, all at knock-down prices. The sheer number of prostitutes working in Bangkok and Pattaya means that it also offers choice in terms of the prostitutes themselves. As one man put it, 'You can go with a different girl every night. It's every man's dream come true'. It is also possible for men to 'experiment' with troilism and, for those who are so inclined, with trans-sexuals and/or underage girls and boys.'

Finally, it should be noted (and this overlaps with points that will be made in the following section) that British men believe their money buys them sexual access to a 'better class' of women in Thailand—'You can take your pick of thousands of the most beautiful women in the world and they're nice girls too. A lot of them are very respectable'.

THE NON-CONTRACTUAL NATURE OF TRANSACTIONS

Although it is the low price of sexual services in Thailand which makes sex tourism a viable activity for so many British men, there is more to their motivation than simply cost considerations. No doubt £ 200 would buy sexual access to almost as many junkies and homeless teenagers in Kings Cross as it does to Thai women but few British sex tourists would consider spending a fortnight in London for that purpose. This is partly because the setting would be colder and not the least 'exotic' and the accommodation and food more expensive, and partly because British street prostitutes are considered to be 'low life' by these men. But it is also because transactions between clients and prostitutes in Britain and in Thailand have a very different character.

In Britain, sexual services are generally sold by the piece and the transaction is modelled on the lines of other commercial exchanges. Like contractual labour in modern, capitalist societies (Littler, 1985), the exchange normally involves an explicit agreement to perform a specified and limited service or task. Obviously, formal contracts are not drawn up, but each party's rights and duties are implicitly defined and generally speaking, in Britain the exchange is so highly focused that the prostitute has fulfilled her side of the contract once the client has ejaculated. An important skill is therefore to be able to bring men to orgasm as quickly as possible, (see O'Connell Davidson, 1994; Hoigard and Finstad, 1992). The narrow and commercial nature of the exchange is more than evident to clients as well as prostitutes and a man would no more expect a prostitute to cuddle or stroke him or act as his companion after sex than he would expect a plumber to do so after fixing a leaking pipe.

There are men who find sexual value in such anonymous and instrumental encounters, but one of the more curious findings of research on prostitution (at least for those who are surprised by the extent of human hypocrisy and capacity for self deceit) is that many sex clients in European countries bemoan the impersonal approach of prostitutes.

De Graaf *et al.* (1992: 9), for example, quote some clients in Amsterdam as saying that they really want comfort, contact and a 'nice chat' from prostitutes and complaining that 'you don't get the warmth and attention that you are looking for'. Hoistad and Fingard (1992: 95) found that although a majority of clients in their Oslo study 'say that they go to a prostitute among other reasons because it is non-committal, they also say that they want warm girls, increased intimacy, and understanding'.

In other words, many men want to buy sex as a commodity but do not want the exchange to be simply a contractual market one. Just as capitalist employers would ideally like employees who are disposable at will, yet wholly devoted, bound to them by pre-market codes of loyalty and allegiance and willing to do more than just stick rigidly to a job description, nirvana for many sex clients would be access on demand to the full range of sexual, emotional and other services from women in exchange for nothing more than a pre-set sum of money.

That European prostitutes are often able to use the rational, economic principles of a free market society to limit and control how much of their sexual and other labour is alienated in exchange for a given fee is a sign of their relative social and economic strength and this becomes clear when their experience is compared to that of most Thai prostitutes.

In Thailand, transactions between clients and prostitutes are far less explicitly contractual. Although men can and do buy 'short time' with prostitutes, giving a predetermined sum of money for a more or less set period of time, the exchange between prostitutes and clients is typically far more diffuse and open ended than that which takes place in Britain.

So far as overnight deals are concerned, the sum of money which the man will pay directly to the prostitute is not always negotiated in advance and the services which the prostitute will provide are rarely explicitly stated.

Moreover, these deals are seldom a simple, focussed exchange of *sexual* services for money. Prostitutes also provide other forms of labour. They often act as companion and interpreter, shop, carry luggage, tidy and clean the client's room, wash and fold his clothes, for example, as well as providing personal services such as massages and manicures.

With 'long haul' deals, women are likewise expected to provide both sexual and non-sexual services but the terms of the exchange are usually even more varied, vague and ill specified than those associated with 24 hour deals. One sex tourist described his three week arrangement as follows:

I started off going a bit crazy, but then I thought I'd just settle with this one girl. I liked her so I told her how much money I'd got left for me holiday and I said to her I could give her 350 Balit a day, and she could do all my shopping, sort out the hotels and laundry and that, and then any money I've got left over at the end of my stay, she can keep it. She was dead pleased with that, and she's really got some bargains, so I'll be able to leave her quite a bit extra.

Another man explained how he had spent two weeks with a woman the previous year, during which time he covered all expenses, bought her several gifts and gave her 'pocket money'. Once back in England, he sent her £ 50. She then wrote to tell him that she had given up bar prostitution and moved back to the countryside, and asked him to pay for a buffalo for her family.

Before parting with the necessary £ 200, the man asked a friend of his who was about to visit Pattaya to check that she had really left the Pattaya bar and was no longer working as prostitute. When his friend confirmed her story, he paid for the buffalo and arranged to spend the whole three weeks of his next holiday with her, again on terms that were essentially left to his discretion rather than negotiated in advance. Walker's (1992) collection of 'love' letters to Bangkok bar prostitutes from western men reveal that such stories are by no means uncommon.

Three points need to be made about all this. First of all, the fact that sex tourists exercise so much control over how much they pay a prostitute and get so much more for what they do pay than they would from British prostitutes is obviously, in itself, very pleasing to them. A Macho Lad commented:

It's up to you what you give the girl; I've give 300, I've give a 1,000. It's up to you. It depends how much you've had to drink... They say 'you give me what you want'. I don't think there's ever a set price for it.

His friend also observed that 'getting the girl' for a whole night made the experience very different from 'going with English prostitutes':

There's no pressure, you can take your time, you don't have to do it straight away and you can do it as much as you like. With some of the girls anyway. It depends a bit. But they're all much more friendly, they really want to please you.

Second, the client experiences his power over the prostitute in a different way in Thailand. The reality is that in Thailand as much as in Britain, the sex client, like all individuals in capitalist societies, 'carries his social power, as also his connection with society, in his pocket' (Marx, 1973: 94). But because he does not have to explicitly agree a price for every service the Thai prostitute provides, she appears to him as acquiescent and subordinate to his whims and desires in a way that a British prostitute never could.

The third point follows from this, and it is that the non-contractual nature of the prostitute-client exchange in Thailand serves to conceal its commercial nature from the man. This aspect of Thai prostitution is absolutely central to most sex tourists, for it makes it possible for them to pay for sexual services without having to see themselves as the kind of men who use prostitutes.

I have no empirical data to support this claim, but I would suggest that though hundreds of thousands of men do use prostitutes, very few willingly and happily embrace the identity of a purchaser-of-sex. To visit a prostitute on occasion may be a sign of machismo but to be dependent on the services of prostitutes because you are unable to 'pull' women is a sign of failure, and the line between the two is a dangerously fine one, especially for men who do not conform to their society's ideals of physical attractiveness.

Certainly, the Mr. Average type does not wish to see himself as a purchaser of sex. Pattaya is 'fantasy island' precisely because when a 22 years old woman approaches him and puts a slim arm around the rolls of fat bulging over the waistband of his trousers or strokes his balding head and tells him that he is 'a sexy man', he can convince himself that it is true. He can suspend his disbelief. In the mirror of the 'beautiful Oriental girl' he sees himself reflected back as half his size and half his age.

But it is not just Mr. Average who is keen to avoid acknowledging the commercial nature of his transactions. Macho Lads and Cosmopolitan Men also stress the fact that Thai prostitutes are not like prostitutes and therefore, it follows that they themselves are not like purchasers-of-sex:

Over here they're not low life like English prostitutes... You don't really think of them as prostitutes.

You don't feel as if you're going with a prostitute, it's not like that. They're more like girlfriends really. You do everything with them. It isn't just sex, they're not like prostitutes.

They really look after you. They make you feel special. You don't feel like a, I don't know how to put it, you don't feel like a customer. They're very natural, very genuine, you can tell that they do really like you.

Because sex tourists do not have to enter into explicit agreements on the terms and conditions of the exchange and because Thai prostitutes make gestures and provide services which are interpreted as demonstrations of genuine affection, it is relatively easy for men to forget that they are engaged in an economic transaction. This in turn helps them to delude themselves into thinking that they have really 'scored', that their personal charms and not their wallets have attracted the woman in question.

Given that the vast majority of British (in fact of all European) sex tourists are less than appealing in terms of European cultural norms of male beauty, it is not difficult to see that sex tourism can do something more for these men's self image than simply make them feel all right about using prostitutes.

The following sections examine the ways in which sex tourism helps British men to reinforce and construct a powerful and positive image of themselves as a particular kind of white heterosexual man.

SEX TOURISM AND MASCULINITY

Segal (1990: 123) has observed that 'masculinity is not some type of single essence, innate or acquired', rather there are competing and contradictory representations of masculinity in western culture. She continues:

> 'Masculinity' is a quality of being which is always incomplete, and which is equally based on a social as on a psychic reality. It exists in the various forms of power men ideally possess: the power to assert control over women, over other men, over their own bodies, over machines and technology.

I want to argue that if the words 'machines and technology' are substituted with 'material objects', then British sex tourists find in their sex tourism the opportunity to become truly 'masculine'. Because the economic power of British men of all social classes is far greater in Thailand than it is in Britain, sex tourists (like all tourists) obtain control over the material world in ways that are not open to them at home.

They can buy rounds of drinks carelessly, eat in smart restaurants and stay in smart hotels, they can indulge in

Dallas and Dynasty fantasies as they sit by swimming pools, waited on hand and foot, they can rent big motorbikes, travel to and from the airport in air conditioned limousines, they can buy cheap silk shirts and fancy leather boots. The life style that at home is reserved only for rich and powerful men is temporarily within their grasp, and as a British observer, one cannot help but be struck by the strutting and swaggering confidence of men who, in their own country, exhibit so little of it.

Obviously these men obtain power over women as well as over the material world (because, of course, women have been reduced to material objects). As one sex tourist put it: There's no pressure on you there, you don't have to worry about going out and getting someone, because you know any time, day or night, you can have anyone you want within seconds. You feel so powerful, you feel you're in control of your sex life.

Unless it is assumed that all men have some kind of biological drive to sexually possess as many women as possible (a view which sex tourists, along with sociobiologists, adhere to) then it is necessary to explain why these particular men have such a strong desire for this kind of control. Almost all the sex tourists interviewed spoke with great bitterness about white women's power to deny them sexual access. Macho Lads complained that English women are 'hard work', that going to discos in England is 'a waste of time', Mr. Average bemoaned the fact that 'pretty' English women know they are pretty and demand the world (they want to marry you then soak you for every penny when they divorce you) and a Cosmopolitan Man told me that:

I'm forty-eight, I'm balding, I'm not as trim as I was. Would a charming, beautiful, young woman want me in England? No. I'd have to accept a big, fat, ugly woman. That's all I could get.

In short, sex tourists express a kind of misogynous rage against women who have the power to demand anything at all—whether it is the right to have a say over who they have sex with and when or the right to maintenance payments for their children. Psychodynamic theories which view all eroticism as an expression of infantile rage, revenge and hostility (see, for example, Stoller, 1979) might explain these men's particular passion for women who are perceived as powerless and sexually available through reference to childhood experiences of rejection and humiliation.

However, one could equally well argue that there is nothing very individual or distinctive about these particular men's attitudes and desires; it is just that they are less well equipped (in terms of economic power, physical appearance and/or social skills) to achieve the degree of access to British women that they would like.

As well as attaining power over the material world and over women, these men experience a greater sense of power over their own bodies in Thailand, certainly so far as their sexuality is concerned. The sex tourist quoted above said that he was 'in control of his sex life', and told me he needed penetrative sex to 'get me sex drive out for the night'. In fact, all the sex tourists I interviewed imagined themselves to be at the mercy of a biological imperative to regularly ejaculate inside a woman's vagina, and the fact that they enjoy sexual access on demand in Thailand is thus interpreted as a form of power over their own bodies. Sex tourism also frees men from other aspects of the body's control over them.

Cultural definitions of beauty turn many people's bodies into prisons, making their sexual desires unattainable, and it is certainly the case that large numbers of sex tourists are either physically repellent by European standards (I have never seen so many enormously overweight men together in one place before), or disfigured or disabled in some way, or too old to be considered sexually attractive.

Finally, sex tourism gives sex tourists a sense of power over other men. The fact that they are in a position to have sex with as many 'beautiful' women as they want makes them feel 'one up' on the men who stay at home. They also engage in a kind of 'ranking' process in relation to other male sex tourists, one which, as the following section shows, allows them to place themselves on the top of a sexualised and 'racialised' scale.

THE CONSTRUCTION OF A WHITE HETEROSEXUAL IDENTITY

One of the more unexpected characteristics of the sex tourist is that he appears to be obsessed by the morality of other sex tourists. At first this appears to be simply an extreme form of hypocrisy. It is acceptable for them, as heterosexual men, to exploit the economic misfortunes of Thai women, but homosexual men who do the same thing to Thai men are 'sick'.

It is acceptable for them to pay a bar fine and take a 16 years old girl back to their hotel for the night, but they expressed a desire to do physical violence to men who pay pimps to take 14 or 15 years old boys back to their rooms. Their own observations of paedophiles, 'gays' and 'perverts' forms an endlessly diverting topic for conversation between themselves and serves as a platform from which to assert their own moral superiority.

In practice this obsession with morality is, I would argue, an obsession with defining and preserving a particular masculine, heterosexual identity, for the moral issue at the heart of their conversations is not whether there can be genuine consent between people who are unequal in terms of age or economic power but whether sex tourists' actions transgress rules about 'normal' male sexuality. This is well illustrated by the following story told to me by a sex tourist from Newcastle:

> When I was in Ko Chang there was this old Austrian bloke, must have been 70 at least, and he was enticing the dogs into his beach hut, tempting stray dogs in there with food. It was fucking disgusting. Anyway, someone told the police and they had words with him, but I was telling this bloke at the bar one night and I pointed the bloke out to him and he just walked over to the Austrian bloke and punched him in the face. He said 'You dirty fucking poofter' and he floored him. He says to me after, 'He comes to paradise and what does he do? Fucks dogs'.

The 'natural' and morally proper thing to do in 'paradise' is, of course, to have sex with a debt-bonded sixteen years old girl in a room above the bar where night after night she must pull strings of razor blades from her vagina in front of an audience of leering men.

But the construction of moral hierarchies by British sex tourists is not only about reinforcing a particular kind of male heterosexual identity. It is also about reinforcing and constructing a specifically white identity. The most powerful venom and moral condemnation is directed towards sex tourists from the Gulf states.

Every sex tourist I spoke to, with the exception of a couple of 'Cosmopolitan Men', told me that Thai women hate 'the Arabs' and avoid 'going with them'. This is because 'Arabs', unlike European men, rape them, cheat them, refuse to pay them, do 'depraved things' to them, insist on anal intercourse, and because 'Arabs' are 'dirty', 'smelly', 'do it with boys and girls', 'hold hands with each other in the streets' and are unattractive to Thai women because they are not white skinned.

In Pattaya, I was even confronted by the extraordinary sight of a British skinhead sitting at a bar with one arm around a Thai woman and the other raised in a Sieg Heil salute at a passing citizen of the Arab Emirates. There is also a British owned bar which proudly displays a poster of a pig wearing a yashmak above which is written. We respect your religion that's why we refuse to serve you'.

Colonial ideologies did and still do express complex and variable forms of racism (see Thomas, 1994), and British sex tourists construct a positive image of themselves as white men not only through the denigration of 'Arabs', but also through their exoticisation and idealisation of Thai women. For these men, Thai women are definitely 'Other', but not the same kind of Other as 'Arab' men or even African Caribbean women (see Collins, 1990; Hooks, 1981; Kovel, 1984; Beckles, 1989).

Thai women are believed to think differently and to have different values and expectations to white women. They' are also held to be more affectionate, loyal, innocent and natural than white women. Thai women are also uniformly held to be great beauties. 'They're all like film stars or models, aren't they? It's the hair and the skin, and they're mostly always petite, you know, slim and small'.

The destructive consequences of 'racist' constructions of Thai women as Other are most immediate and most terrifying around issues of safer sex.

All the men I interviewed commented on how clean Thai women are, noting things like the frequency with which 'They' wash. 'Their' neat and tidy appearance. 'Their' scrupulously clean and manicured nails and so on. The implications of this were spelled out clearly by one man:

I don't know why people always go on about AIDs in Thailand. Thai women are the cleanest women in the world. They don't shower once a day, they don't shower twice a day. They shower four times a day.

His friend, who also appeared to believe that frequent washing is a prophylactic against. AIDS, told me that 'most of the girls will do it without a condom if you pay them enough', but that he would never have unprotected sex with a bar girl, only with freelances who seemed new to the work.

Romanticised views of Thai women as 'innocent', 'natural', 'clean' and so on exist alongside an implicit denigration of Thai men, for British sex tourists are convinced that, despite their own 'exotic' charm and beauty, Thai women recognise the superiority of whites. Sex tourists continually assert that Thai women prefer white men (white skin "turns them on', white men 'treat them better than Arabs and their own kind') and that Thai women would actually like to be white themselves 'They admire white skin,' 'They won't sunbathe because they want to be white', 'Basically, they all want to get married to a European').

There are some interesting parallels between contemporary British sex tourists' beliefs about Thai women and nineteenth century Britons' beliefs about Black women in the Caribbean. Beckles (1989:148) quotes a visitor to Barbados in the 1820s:

> Generally speaking, the [coloured women] look down... with a feeling of contempt on men of their own colour... and rather than live with them a virtuous and inoffensive life, they prefer dwelling with a white man in a state of moral degradation.

So far as sex tourists today are concerned, such beliefs help them to explain to themselves why young and beautiful Thai women find them so irresistible without having to refer to the commercial side of their relationship, and thus to further deflect attention from their identity as purchasers of sex. But they also link into other self serving stereotypes, especially those surrounding the supposed subservient, passive and accommodating nature of Thai and other 'oriental' women.

For as well as attributing the characteristics already mentioned to Thai women, sex tourists are of the opinion that Thai women are genetically and culturally predisposed towards subordination and self-denial.

Through the lens of their 'racism', these men interpret virtually everything that Thai women do as a mark of their desire to serve. If a British man holds a door open for a British woman, it is not interpreted as a mark of his subjugation to her. But when Thai women observe certain formal codes governing respect for and the care of others (for instance, speaking in a low voice, paying attention to a companion's physical comfort and so on), it is taken to be a mark of her willing subjection. British sex tourists tell you that 'it's in their nature to be subservient' or that 'it's part of their culture', and this is why prostitutes will carry their bags and suitcases, clean their combs, pour their drinks, plump up their pillows and so on.

They also view Thai women as sexually passive, using terms like 'innocent' and 'natural' to describe their sexuality. 'They aren't into anything kinky' one man told me, and those who use prostitutes in Britain claim that Thai prostitutes seem inexperienced; 'English prostitutes know all the tricks, they take the lead, they suggest things. But Thai girls are very innocent, they're very natural and affectionate'. These qualities are described as 'a big turn on to British men, and it is also conveniently assumed that 'innocent' Thai women thoroughly enjoy straight, penetrative sex with them (which is, of course, partly why they don't like 'perverted Arabs').

All variants of 'racism' serve to deny the subjectivity and humanity of those defined as Other, and Ward (1988:28) points out that this denial can 'be constituted through a process of idealisation' as much as through one of denigration. Certainly the idealised 'innocence' of Thai women appears to serve the same purpose as the attribution of 'voracious' sexual appetites to Brazilian women by sex tourists in San Paulo (and the attribution of 'libidinous' and 'animalistic' sexuality to Black women by whites in slave societies of the Caribbean). For whether she is constructed as passive and innocent or active and depraved, the Other is imagined to relish the white man's sexual attentions.

But it is also important to note that, even so far as any one 'racialised' group is concerned, there is a certain plasticity about these processes of denial, and the 'racialised' world view of British sex tourists in Thailand can serve ends other than those described so far. For although a majority of the sex tourists I interviewed were primarily interested in penetrating the vaginas of 'beautiful' and subservient women, there were some, particularly Macho Lads, whose sexual interests were more wide ranging.

Again, their 'racism' helped them to feel all right about their desires and activities. It has already been observed that sex tourists draw very sharp boundaries between the 'natural' and 'unnatural', the 'normal' and the 'perverse', and that these boundaries also mark off masculinity. Men who transgress them are not 'real men'. Yet several Macho Lads admitted to engaging in sexual practices in Thailand that they would normally define as 'perverse'. For example, 'sharing' a Thai prostitute with male friends, allowing male friends to video them having sex with a prostitute, and having sexual contact with trans-sexual prostitutes.

Patterson (1982: 51) has observed that where caste relations 'demarcate impassable boundaries', the essence of slavery is that 'the slave, in his social death, lives on the margins between... life and death, the sacred and the secular. Already dead, he lives outside the manna of the gods and can cross the boundaries with social and supernatural impunity' and for some British sex tourists, it appears that Thai sex workers, as 'racialised' Others, have this kind of liminal status. They have so little social worth that it is possible for the sex tourist to transgress boundaries and do things which, if done with a white person, would bring dishonour. As one Macho Lad said:

> I was in this bar, a no-hands bar, and this girl, well except she was a fella, a Lady Boy, come up and did a blow job... I knew she was a he, you can always tell by the Adam's apple. But I didn't really care. It's all right here. But I'd slit my throat if that happened in England.

CONTRADICTIONS IN THE WORLD VIEW OF THE SEX TOURIST

It should be evident from the above discussion that the world view of the British sex tourist is not wholly internally consistent, and that his desires are often self-contradictory. He wants Thai women to be both sexually available and sexually innocent, and although sex tourists say that they like the 'subservience' of Thai women, they also complain about their 'passivity'. Several men told me that they often 'got sick of the compliance of the women whose bodies and labour they purchase. As one said:

> It gets on your nerves after a while, whatever you ask, they say 'It's up to you'. 'Do you want the telly on?', 'Up to you'. 'Do you want something to eat?', 'Up to you'. 'Shall we stop at this bar?', 'Up to you'. 'Do you want to make love?', 'Up to you'. It drives you mad.

Meanwhile, a general complaint about 'long haul' deals is that it is very difficult to build a relationship with the woman because of language problems and the absence of a shared culture. In fact, many sex tourists say that they get lonely for their 'own kind' whilst on holiday in Thailand. As one Cosmopolitan Man explained:

> I could never be happy in a relationship with a Thai woman. They aren't intellectual, they don't read, they've

nothing to say. Life's always a compromise. You can talk to western women, but they don't look good. With Thai girls it's the other way round, so you always have to take the rough with the smooth. Life's never perfect.

Oddly enough, many sex tourists are actually also troubled by moral issues surrounding consent. These men generally know that Thailand is a 'poor country' and that many women are forced to prostitute themselves in order to support their families. On the one hand, this helps them to sustain the notion that Thai prostitutes are not really prostitutes (and thus that they are not really buyers of sex). These women do not conform to their stereotypes of prostitutes and can be considered as 'decent' and 'respectable' women who just unfortunately happen to live in a country where poverty drives them to sell their bodies. But in recognising this, their own actions come to seem morally reprehensible.

It looks dangerously as though they are taking advantage of the misfortunes of these, damsels in distress. Now Macho Lads are not much troubled by this. They tend to view sex tourism almost as a form of welfare provision by the West for an economically 'backward' nation—'If these blokes stopped coming out here, I'd hate to think what would happen to these girls', as one remarked. But for Mr. Average, who wants so much to see himself as a 'decent' bloke, it is a real dilemma.

The easiest way to resolve it is to tell himself that the 'beautiful girl' in his bed is there because she finds him so desirable, not because her poverty has forced her there. But such a fiction is hard to maintain when Mr. Average is daily confronted by the sight of 'beautiful girls', perhaps his own former sexual partners, telling other, often still less attractive Europeans that they too are 'sexy men'.

There is always a tension for Mr. Average between seeing himself as truly desired and so feeling good about himself, and seeing himself as exploiting 'nice, respectable girls' and feeling bad about himself. Some men become defensive in response to this.

A number of Mr. Averages expressed great ambivalence towards prostitutes, lurching irrationally from paternalistic sympathy—'They do it for their families'—to malevolent hostility -'They're hard bitches really' in the space of only a few minutes conversation.

I was assured that despite all appearances to the contrary, most of the bar girls in Pattaya were actually earning huge sums of money and frittering it away instead of saving for a rainy day'. 'You buy them gold and the moment you leave, they just sell it and spend the money', one complained. 'You must never fall in love, or they'll skin you alive' another warned.

Perhaps the most unpleasant Mr. Average of all was the one who sat down with me in the hotel lobby one morning, still drunk from the night before, three days growth of stubble on his face, his shirt and trousers stained with food and said:

It's all changed here.

You never saw a girl drink or smoke when I first came to Thailand. All the business with whisky and cigarettes is totally new.

They were nice girls then. They were soft, very soft. Now it's all changed. It's commercialism.

They're hard and they be after money.

CHILD PROSTITUTION AND SEX TOURISM—CUBA

In Cuba, the link between tourism and prostitution is perhaps more direct than in any other country which hosts sex tourists. Although the sexual exploitation of women and children by colonists, slave holders and neocolonial elites had been a constant theme of the island's history, the post 1959 Cuban state made a sustained and successful attempt to wipe out the organised basis of prostitution. Indeed, for some commentators, this represents one of the greatest achievements of the Revolution. Randall (1974: 237), for example, opens a chapter in her book on Cuban women thus:

> Cuba: Vice capital of the Caribbean! Cuba: Free Territory in America!
>
> The "before" and "after", translated into lives... a woman who once sold her body to feed her children is now a teacher, a nurse, a secretary, cane-cutter or bookstore clerk... for the woman who was a prostitute, 1959 wrought the most dramatic change of all.

It must be borne in mind that the revolutionary state had to contend with the economic legacy of colonialism, slavery and underdevelopment, as well as with intense hostility from the United States of America, the world's leading economic power and although it sought to address the social and economic conditions which had previously underpinned the supply of prostitutes, it was hardly in a position to completely transform them. In this sense, its success in eradicating prostitution probably rested heavily upon the elimination of effective demand for commercial sex. Wealthy Cubans fled the country (as did many of the 'underworld' characters who had previously promoted and organised the kind of prostitution that serves a poorer clientele), and wealthy foreign 'playboys' no longer visited it.

In the 1980s, however, a series of events threw the Cuban economy into crisis (see Stubbs, 1989) and the state had little alternative but to respond to this by developing its tourist industry. With mass tourism came large scale effective demand for prostitution. Since many Cuban people are currently experiencing enormous economic hardship, it is not surprising that a supply of prostitutes has emerged to meet this demand.

A more general description of the phenomenon of sex tourism in Cuba and the way in which prostitution is organised there has already been provided by one of the authors (see O'Connell Davidson, 1995) and we have also written in some detail about the organisation of child prostitution in Cuba (see O'Connell Davidson and Sanchez Taylor, 1996). In this report, we are more specifically concerned with the experience of child prostitutes in Cuba and the identity and motivations of their clients. For the purposes of this document, 'children' will be defined as individuals below the age of sexual consent in Cuba, i.e. under 16 years of age. After briefly noting some methodological issues and problems, we provide some information about child prostitutes and then move on to present profiles of the tourists who exploit them.

METHODOLOGICAL ISSUES

Fieldwork in Cuba was undertaken by Julia O'Connell Davidson and Jacqueline Sanchez Taylor in August 1995. The project built upon fieldwork undertaken in March of the same year, so that the information in this report, and analysis offered, draws on 29 days and nights' research. We made use of ethnographic research techniques (primarily observation and interviewing) and were also able to develop research relationships with three 'key informants': a 15 years old girl who will be referred to as Anna-Bel, a 21 years old prostitute woman who will be referred to as Lola and a 20 years old prostitute man who will be referred to as Rudolpho.

Through these informants we were able to develop links with a network of around 20 teenage prostitutes (aged between 13 and 20) working in the beach resort of Varedero. This in turn made it possible for us to 'hang out' with them in their place of work, observing the ways in which sex tourists interacted with them and interviewing them about their clients on a number of different occasions. Our repeated presence in the same bar and our relationship with this group of prostitutes also made it possible to identify and interview a group of 'regular' sex tourists who are known to local prostitutes for their sexual preference for children.

A coincidence further enriched the data we were able to gather. In March, we had visited Santiago de Cuba where our hotel room was robbed by a girl (Gretchen) to whom we had been chatting. The hotel security caught her and we ended up having to spend several hours in the police station with Gretchen and her accomplice. The police interviewed the two girls and look their statements whilst we were in the room, which meant that we knew, among other things, exactly how old they were —15 and 13. On our second field trip we met these same two girls in Varedero (some 700 km from their home town), where they were working as prostitutes. We were not only able to interview them but also to note the identity of their clients. This meant that we were able to identify more sex tourists who sexually exploit underage children and to approach them for interview.

A key problem that we faced in undertaking this research was the fact that all our interview work (except with trusted key informants) had to be covertly undertaken. Because it seemed unlikely that the Cuban Embassy would issue a work visa to researchers concerned with a topic that is currently viewed as embarrassing to the Cuban state, we entered the country on a tourist visa. This meant that we could not take the simplest route to discovering certain background details about sex tourists (namely, asking them to co-operate with general research on tourism in order to ask a series of questions about age, occupation, other holiday destinations, etc.) but had to conduct all interviews as though they were chance 'conversations'.

Although, the narcissism of the average sex tourist is so great that most appeared unsurprised to find themselves closely interrogated by a total stranger (they clearly thought it only natural that a woman would want to know all about them and few asked any questions at all about why we were so inquisitive, what we did for a living and so on), it was not always possible to steer every conversation around to cover every detail that was required to complete a full data set. Table 1, which provides background information on the 24 sex tourists interviewed is therefore incomplete. It was also the case that some of the sex tourists who had a clear preference for underage girls and were fully conscious of their own criminality became suspicious about us. Their paranoia, and the need to avoid further exacerbating it, also operated as a constraint on our interviewing and observational work.

Despite these problems, we managed to interview 22 men in-depth and to conduct briefer interviews (less than one hour) with a further 12 sex tourists.

As was the case with the report on Costa Rica, we are unable to provide (any reliable information about the scale of the problem of child prostitution in Cuba. It seems probable that, by comparison with Costa Rica, and certainly by comparison with Thailand, the number of children who are sexually exploited in Cuba is small. However, it is also the case that most of the child sexual exploitation that does take place in Cuba is perpetrated by tourists.

THE EXPERIENCE OF CHILD PROSTITUTES IN CUBA

Cuban wages are generally somewhere between 250 and 400 Pesos per month, which may be just about enough to support a very frugal existence when used within the rationed and/or subsidised state economy. But this official economy is rapidly contracting and many basic necessities can only be obtained for hard currency from tourist shops or 'black' market entrepreneurs. In the unofficial economy, the Cuban's Peso income is all but worthless. For large numbers of Cubans, the pursuit of dollars has become a far more meaningful economic activity than that which takes place in formal work settings. Since tourists are the most accessible source of hard currency (it is unsurprising that many adults and children travel to tourist centres in the hope that they will somehow be able to milk tourists for a few of their dollars.

Although such '*nigociacion*' does not necessarily involve commercial sex there are very few women and girls who migrate to tourist areas who do not, at some point, have to resort to prostitution. In the following pages, we highlight key features of migrant child prostitutes' experience through reference to one child's journey in and out of prostitution, a child we will ref to as Anna-Bel.

Anna-Bel is the eldest of five children and had been working as a prostitute in Varadero (Cuba's most established tourist resort) for three months when we first interviewed her in March, 1995. She was then 14 years old. Anna-Bel had returned to her home village by the time of our second trip to Cuba in August 1995 and we visited her there. Anna-Bel comes from a very small village in Ciego de Avila, a poor inland province about 500 km away from Varadero.

Another 14 years old girl from the same village also prostitutes herself in Varedero and Anna-Bel reckoned that at least five girls from her school (which serves three or four such villages) had also worked as prostitutes in Varedero. Anna-Bel's father is a 42 years old agricultural worker who earns around 3 Pesos per month.

Because he works in a co-operative and can obtain certain rationed items within the peso economy, the family is assured a basic subsistence. However, the shortages caused by the US blockade and other economic pressures mean that many staple goods, such as cooking oil, soap, detergent, clothing, shoes, are only available on the 'black' market for dollars. Anna-Bet's father's entire income would only translate into around $100 per month and there is thus no way in which he can furnish a family of six with anything beyond the bare minimum necessary for survival.

The family lives in a three roomed house. Four daughters share one bedroom and the parents and baby share the other. As well as the bedroom there is a dining area, a sitting area and a scullery-style kitchen. Through western eyes, the family has very little furniture and very few personal possessions and the house is neat but bare. There is nothing squalid about the dwelling, yet the family's life is made bleak by the effects of the blockade and Cuba's other economic problems. Flies stream in from the pig sty that stands a couple of meters from the back door, they swarm around the house constantly and settle on food the moment it is placed on the table.

Anna-Bel's mother complains she can do nothing to get rid of them even if fly paper or spray or even net for the windows or doors were available in the shops, they would not be able to afford them. The red dirt of the yard outside turns into mud when it rains and because the weather is humid, it stays tacky for days or weeks. The mud gets everywhere, over the children, over their clothes and over the furniture, and trying to clean it without any kind of detergent is time consuming and demoralising. There is nothing for the children to do. They have no playthings, no paper, no books. The village itself is bleak in the same kind of way. No-one living there does anything but struggle to make ends meet in order to wake the following day and do the same thing all over again.

Before Anna-Bel left for Varedero, her father told her that she should understand how fortunate the family is to have food enough to eat, a roof over their head, even a television that can be watched for an hour or two when the electricity supply is switched on. Other families in Cuba are not so lucky. But Anna-Bel did not feel fortunate. She wanted a pair of shoes that belonged to her and her alone, instead of having to share a pair of white plimsolls with her younger sister, plimsolls that got stained by the red mud the moment she left the house and that had to be scrubbed endlessly in cold water before they could be worn again. She wanted clothes that were not ragged, she wanted shampoo and soap. She wanted to see something different, do something different. She wanted something to happen.

A 16 years old cousin, Isabel, had already visited Varedero once, having been 'recruited' by an older friend. Isabel had a baby and as well as feeling trapped in the same way as Anna-Bel did, she wanted to contribute towards the child's maintenance. She told Anna-Bel that in Varedero, all the things they longed for were readily available and suggested that the two of them could go there, telling her 'All you have to do is go with tourists and they give you dollars and clothes and everything'.

Anna-Bel had no real idea what 'going with a tourist' would involve. Isabel had given her to understand that it referred to something sexual but since Anna-Bel herself had never had sex and had been told very little about it, this was hardly enlightening. Isabel minimised the problems she had encountered on her first trip as she wanted someone to accompany her.

Anna-Bel left the village without telling her parents what she was doing. The two girls hitch-hiked to Varedero, which took them three days, and arrived to find themselves effectively homeless and penniless. Anna-Bel was entirely without experience or knowledge of prostitution and Isabel, despite having spent a month there earlier that year, was hardly worldly wise. In Cuba, it is this, rather than the existence of formal brothel based prostitution, which makes young girls vulnerable to forms of hyper-exploitation.

In the first instance, they are open to exploitation by 'black' market renters. There is a chronic shortage of housing in Cuba and only official residents of any given town or city are entitled to accommodation. Though it is possible to privately own property, it is illegal to rent it out, so that unless people migrate for official work, there is no legitimate way to obtain housing.

Anna-Bel and her cousin managed to find a room to share in a flat with four other girls in Miramar, a town 2 km from Varadero. Each girl paid $1.50 per night to the landlady who also lived in the flat. Other prostitutes we interviewed were paying between $1 and $4 per night, depending upon whether the accommodation was in Varedero itself or in outlying towns or villages. These high rents effectively lock them into prostitution as a means of survival, for there is no alternative means of securing the dollars necessary to pay it.

Young girls who migrate to tourist centres to prostitute themselves are also vulnerable to a form of hyper-exploitation by sex tourists. None of the young girls we interviewed spoke any language other than Spanish and this, in combination with a lack of experience and the confidence that brings, meant that they found it very difficult to negotiate transactions with tourists. Anna-Bel, for example, never contracted to provide specific sexual services and rarely even managed to clearly negotiate a price for her services in advance. Instead, she would accompany tourists back to their hotel rooms, acquiesce to their demands and accept anything that they chose to give her the following morning. In general, they paid her the 'going rate', between $30 and $50 per night, but there had been occasions when tourists had given her nothing at all.

Other under-age girls reported the same problems in negotiating both the terms and the nature of transactions. There are, for example, men whose idea of fun is to get two young girls to 'perform' sexually while they watch, or to set up 'parties' involving four or more people. This was particularly distressing to the under-age prostitutes we interviewed, none of whom knew anything at all about voyeurism or even lesbianism prior to working in Varedero and saw what they were being asked to do as 'unnatural' and horrible. One sex tourist coerces under-age girls into this type of act by threatening to report them to the police for theft if they do not comply with his wishes.

Because many of the younger *jinteras* (Cuban slang for prostitutes, which literally means 'jockey' as women are perceived to be riding tourists) are inexperienced and lack confidence they are often relatively passive in terms of initiating contact with prospective clients. In the bars, these girls tend to spend their time dancing, joking, giggling (sometimes weeping) with each other, trying to catch the attention of male tourists but rarely approaching them directly. This opens the door for yet another variant of third party involvement. Older and more experienced *jinteras* will assume the role of intermediary, effecting introductions and negotiating on the child's behalf, charging a fee for so doing.

Children like Anna-Bel are especially vulnerable to this added layer of exploitation. She is physically very immature, standing about 4'10", with hands and feet the size of a child much younger than her 14 years. She dresses in a childlike fashion which emphasises her diminutive stature and her mannerisms are those of a little girl rather than a teenager.

She is thus ideal fodder for men with a specific sexual interest in just-pubertal girls and older *jinteras* who recognise this type of demand are quick to exploit an acquaintance with girls like this.

Finally, girls like Anna-Bel and her cousin are vulnerable to sexual abuse and economic exploitation by corrupt policemen and by pimps. In Cuba as a whole there is probably less police corruption than in most countries of the world but Varedero is an exceptiónal place and local people say that corruption is widespread. Prostitutes told us that they are frequently intimidated by plain clothes policemen, as well as by their snitches, who demand dollars and/or clothing from them. Stories about sexual intimidation and rape by police are also commonplace, though we only spoke to one prostitute who had herself experienced this.

Meanwhile, though there is very little formal third party involvement in prostitution in Cuba, there are men who pimp on an opportunistic, *ad hoc* basis, generally from within the context of an abusive relationship with the girl concerned.

After Isabel and Anna-Bel had been in Varedero for about a month, for instance, they met up with a man named Yuggi. He is 20 and comes from Varedero where he lives with his family. Yuggi and his two brothers are muscle-bound, bleach haired young men, *jinteras* (masculine equivalent *jinteras*) who help European and North American women to indulge in a Chippendale fantasy whilst on holiday. But much easier money is to be made from girls like Anna-Bel and Isabel.

Yuggi runs a series of relationships with such girls—he was 'dating' Irsabel, Anna-Bel and another 14 years old prostitute from Santiago de Cuba in March and had two freshly arrived 15 years old on the go when we returned in August. He abuses these children in a number of ways:

demanding sex (usually unsafe sex—there is nowhere private for them to go, so such men take the girls into the sea to have sexual intercourse with them); demanding money and physically abusing them. Anna-Bel, for example, was giving Yuggi $10 out of every $20 she made. When she was unable to find clients he beat her.

Isabel was picked up by the police in April. She was tried and sentenced, to four years in prison. The sentence has subsequently been reduced to two years, but she is being held in a prison far from her home village and none of her family has been able to visit her. She will not see her child until it almost three years old. As is the case all over the world, the law punishes prostitutes but seldom intervenes with their clients. We heard a rumour that last year one tourist had been picked up and charged with a sexual offence against an under-age girl.

Given the fact that so many men so openly use child prostitutes in Varedero and that prostitutes and seasoned clients alike will point out the plain clothes policemen 'working' in the bars where these girls solicit, one can only assume that (if the rumour is true) this tourist must have either committed extremely violent crime or have failed to offer the police a sufficiently large inducement to get off (perhaps both).

Yuggi's demands for cash meant that Anna-Bel was unable to save money in Varedero and in April what little she had managed to buy herself in way of clothes was robbed from the apartment in which she was staying. She wanted to go home but felt ashamed to return empty handed, besides which she was unsure how to get home. Eventually, Yuggi beat her so badly that she sent a telegraph to her father asking him to come and collect her. Her father, who had no idea where Anna-Bel was and had lost stone to weigh worrying about her, came immediately to fetch her..

Back in her village, Anna-Bel helps her mother around the home. She has not relumed to school because she has missed too much and failed her exams. She cannot legally work until she is 17. She feels guilty and ashamed of her 'past'. There is no-one to counsel her or help her come to terms with the sexual and physical abuse to which she was subjected in Varedero. She still does not own a pair of shoes.

It comes as no surprise that the well heeled, adult men who go to Cuba to have sexual intercourse with girls like Anna-Bel are indifferent both to the conditions which lead them to prostitution and their suffering as a consequence of it. After all, if they did not dehumanise and objectify such children they would hardly be capable of taking advantage of their misfortunes in this way.

What is perhaps more surprising is the 'party line' on prostitutes currently adopted by the *Federacion de Mujers Cubanas* (FMC), about the only formal organisation in Cuba from which women and children might be able to expect support and aid. This 'line' is so similar to that adopted by right wing western politicians about their own poor, homeless and sexually exploited that it almost beggars belief. *Jiniteras* are accused of having 'low moral values', of being 'greedy' and 'covetous'.

Unlike pre-revolutionary prostitutes who were 'forced' into prostitution in order to subsist or to provide for their children, today's *jiniteras* are 'goodtime girls' in search of easy money. We were told by one party faithful in Varedero that prostitution was a terrible thing because girls like Anna-Bel 'brought shame on Cuba' and 'gave tourists a bad impression' of Cuban women. The fact that around 80% of the tourists to Varedero visit the town only because they are actively seeking opportunities to sexually exploit other people's economic misfortunes appeared to have escaped her entirely.

One of the most painful things to learn about the Cuban women and girls who prostitute themselves to tourists is that most of them internalise their society's view of them as immoral, superficial and worthless. Thus, while sex tourists tell you how wonderfully sexually permissive Cuban culture is, women like Lola (a 21 years old who wants to be able to buy clothes, toys and books for her four years old daughter and to buy a home so that both she and her daughter can have a bedroom each instead of sharing one in her own parent's home) tell you that they hope one day to find a respectable Cuban man to marry them, someone who will cleanse them of their 'stain' and ensure that their children will not have to carry their 'shame'.

While sex tourists tell you how 'natural' and 'uninhibited' these girls are, 15 years old get crying drunk in bars and tell you that they are *'chicas malas,'* and that no-one will ever be able to love them. The very ambiguity of these girls' status, *jiniteras* rather than professional *putas* (whores or bitches)—an ambiguity which most sex tourists find very pleasing— increases the guilt and anxiety associated with sex work.

Recognising prostitution as a 'job' and taking a business-like approach to it protects the woman's self esteem to some degree by making quite transparent the fact that the acts she performs with or for clients has absolutely nothing to do with her own sexuality. A prostitute who fails to self-identify as a prostitute is left with an extremely undermining view of herself; instead of seeing herself as a person making a rational choice out of an invidious bunch of alternatives, she runs the risk of beginning to believe herself to be all those things which clients attribute to her—promiscuous, sexually indiscriminate, hypersexual, immoral.

We interviewed more than forty prostitute women and children in the course of two field trips to Cuba, and almost all of them recounted life stories which were tragic in themselves. Especially poignant is the case of a 23 years old mother of a disabled child who came to Varedero to prostitute herself in the hope of being able to save enough money to buy a decent home and enough clothing for him. While she was there, her son died. No-one knew how to contact her and she returned home to Las Tunas after a month to find he had been buried two weeks earlier.

The idea that on top of everything else, these women and children recriminate themselves and imagine themselves to be somehow dirtied and debased is unbearable. Indeed, there are ways in which the psychological impact of this form of prostitution seems to resemble that of incestuous abuse. The young girls we interviewed saw themselves as complicit in ways which made them feel intensely guilty, for example. Their sense of complicity is reinforced by the doublespeak of the FMC and of the sex tourists themselves, a doublespeak which attributes 'agency' to the powerless party and absolves the powerful party of all responsibility, calling teenage girls 'temptresses' and adult men their 'victims'.

There are some child prostitutes who are less painfully naive than Anna-Bel and who, in this sense, perhaps partially match the FMC's description of them. The girls who robbed us in Santiago, for instance, are hardly exemplars of self-disciplined socialist virtuosity. In Varedero, they were continuing to supplement their earnings from prostitution with theft and it may well be true that their value system is one which places possession of fashionable clothing above other more collective, noble or spiritual aspirations.

But it is also true that it is wealthy men many years their senior who take advantage of these 'values' and that while these men walk away from encounters with such teenagers swaggering, satisfied and entirely free of the threat of prosecution, the girls display all the same behavioural symptoms that sexually abused children the world over display: anxiety, depression, an obsessive interest in their own sexuality, low self esteem, etc.

The idea that the only 'protection' their society can offer them is a period of imprisonment and 're-education' is almost as obscene as the idea that the imprisonment of their abusers is unlikely and the 're-education' of such men is not even on any government's agenda.

So far as the prostitution of prepubertal children in Cuba goes, we are unable to provide any reliable information. Many of the conditions which allow sex tourists to abuse prepubertal children in other countries exist in Cuba—poverty, private accommodation, corrupt officials etc., and it is not uncommon to find adult Cubans (who usually claim to be the child's relative) using young children to beg on tourist beaches. We heard many rumours to the effect that such people also sell sexual access to these children, but found it difficult to substantiate them.

We interviewed a man in his 50s who was begging with a child of nine years. He told us that such things happen but denied having ever sold his niece to tourists. The little girl also spoke to us and told us that she had many tourist 'friends', all of whom were male. She said that she sometimes visited them in their apartments and that an Italian man had once given her and her uncle a present of $70.

The presence of her uncle made it impossible to press her for details about these 'friendships'. The most we can say is that it seems likely that this kind of abuse does occur.

We are also unable to provide reliable information about the sexual exploitation of male children. We heard rumours about male homosexual tourists sexually exploiting teenage boys but did not observe any such men with Cuban children. This lack of visibility could be because homosexuality is heavily stigmatised in Cuba (it is still illegal to publicly display homosexuality), but if this were the case, it would make Cuba an unlikely destination for the homosexual sex tourist.

'Rudolpho' told us that when he first arrived in Varedero at the age of 16 he had a two week long sexual 'relationship' with a Canadian woman of 62. However, while there are a small number of female sex tourists in Cuba, the women we observed were all with men in their early twenties rather than with children.

PROFILES OF SEX TOURISTS WHO USE UNDER-AGE PROSTITUTES IN CUBA

The background characteristics of the sex tourists we interviewed in Cuba are shwon in Table 1. The age range was from 22 to 68 and the majority of this sample occupy relatively privileged socio-economic positions in their home countries. Over 90 per cent of them were on return visits to Cuba and three quarters of those asked had also visited other well-known sex tourist destinations such as the Dominican Republic, Thailand and the Philippines. Around two-thirds of them were staying in private accommodation rather than in hotels.

Out of a sample of 24 men, we know with reasonable certainty that 13 had, had sex with under-age girls while holidaying in Cuba (we take as certain those cases where the man actually admitted this to us or where we both observed them behaving in a proprietorial way with girls we knew to be underage and asked the girls to confirm that the man had actually purchased her 'services').

In other words, we are sure that 38% of our sample had sexually exploited girls under the age of 16. This sample cannot be used to make generalisations about the percentage of all sex tourists who use under-age girls since we were specifically trying to find and interview men who do have a sexual interest in young girls. Profiles of some of the sex tourists we interviewed are provided here.

Jake

Jake is a 46 year old unmarried Canadian from Montreal who spends most of his time living in Latin America and the Caribbean. He funds his wanderings in two main ways: by writing magazine articles and books on diet and fitness for women and by running cigars between Cuba and Canada. He clearly considers himself to be both set apart from and a cut above his fellow countrymen. Canada and the States are, he says, 'TV land' and the mass of the people there are unintelligent, superficial and materialistic.

Unlike them, he is a youthful 'free spirit'. He displays this to the world through various ludicrous affectations—striding into the sea to swim without taking off either his clothes or his 'bum-bag, for example. He appears to be inordinately anxious about his own ageing. He wears his hair peroxided, permed and shoulder length, carries the kind of fashion accessories that are popular with people 20 years his junior and is obsessed by the marks of ageing upon other people.

Like many other sex tourists, Jake believes that sexual mores are very different in 'the third world' where people are 'free' and 'natural' about their sexuality. He explains this 'difference' in the following way:

Kids grow up with sex here and know it's a calming and good thing. They sleep ten to a room, so children hear their parents fuck... subconsciously they know it's a good thing. They associate it with a release... tension builds up, then their parents fuck, and everything is OK.

According to Jake, women and girls in 'the Third World' are 'natural' and 'in tune with their bodies'. In Cuba the girls 'come from the jungle with no shoes... they'd fuck on the streets if it wasn't for the police'. He told one of the authors, a black woman, that the fact she had no wish to take up his invitation to 'fuck' him demonstrated that she had 'lost touch with her roots'. The same generous offer was not extended to the other author, a white woman, whose biology clearly 'rooted' her in a non-sexual world.

As an ageing hippie, Jake's beliefs about his own and other people's sexuality are linked to a set of ideas about 'healthy, natural living' and the release of 'tension'—he refers to his nightly sexual exploitation of prostitute women as 'getting a massage', for instance.

In effect, this 'alternative medicine' model produces a view of male sexuality accepted by a majority of sex tourists—a belief that men's physical well being is endangered if they are unable to penetrate women's vaginas on demand.

As with other sex tourists we have interviewed, Jake enjoys the sense of freedom and control which his economic power brings him in 'Third World' countries. This power not only enables him to live well in terms of housing, food, entertainment etc., but also allows him to reduce other human beings to mere objects. When his offer of sex was turned down by the aforementioned author, for instance, he attempted to make the proposition more 'interesting' in the following way:

You don't want to fuck me? How'd you like to watch me fuck another girl? You can come along and watch. You don't have to do anything, just watch. Pick a girl, any girl, any size, any colour, pick any girl you like.

As he said this, he gestured around the bar toward Cuban women and girls as if they were but commodities in a supermarket. His money gives him the power to command their bodies, even if only to be used as a vehicle for sexual access to another, momentarily more desirable, woman.

James

James is a 48 years old Canadian. He teaches in an engineering department of a college in Ontario and is referred to by his male sex tourist friends as 'the professor'. He is unmarried and spends his annual three month summer vacation travelling in 'Third World ountries' and practising sex tourism. He had previously visited Thailand, the Philippines, Vietnam, Cambodia and a number of Latin American countries.

This year he had 'done' the Trans-Siberian Express and spent a month in China before coming to Cuba to 'recuperate' for two weeks. It was his fifth visit to Cuba.

James does not see himself as a client even though he gives money to the girls and women with whom he has sexual intercourse. 'There's a big difference between making a business deal with a prostitute and meeting someone you like, talking to each other and then hopping into bed', he told us. James describes himself as a 'gentleman' and he maintains and develops this image of himself through the denigration of 'Third World' men.

Unlike him and other white men, Cuban men abuse their women and children. They are physically violent and do not treat women as 'ladies'. This is all 'down to Latin machismo', he explained.

James styles himself as a 'funny-man'. He sits in bars surrounded by prostitute women and children and 'clowns about'. He affects deafness so that the girls have to lean closer to speak to him, at which point he touches their bottoms and then pretends that it was someone else who touched them; he walks around the bar with the stilted movements of an automaton; he performs conjuring tricks with coins and serviettes; he blows up balloons and fashions them into the shape of a penis.

It is the kind of 'joking around' that, when less overtly sexual, adults often imagine that children enjoy. James told me that back in Canada people think he is a bit of an 'eccentric' but describe him as 'good with children'. In Cuba, his delight in this childish world can be more given a more direct expression. The prostitute he 'dated' on the nights we observed him was 15 years old.

Bruce, John and Mark

Bruce, John and Mark are a group of Canadians, all in their 40s, who make between four and five trips per year to Cuba, flying directly from Toronto or Montreal to Varedero. None of them could be described as short of money (Bruce works in a motor company as an electrical designer and owns two houses, two cars and a boat; Mark is a semi-retired real estate dealer) but they fund their frequent trips to Cuba by smuggling clothing, watches and jewellery from Canada into Cuba and Cuban cigars back into Canada.

These men stay in *cases particulars* rather than hotels in Varedero and have several Cuban friends who are active on the 'black' market with whom they do business. Mark and John's sexual tastes are known to local male hustlers who procure young girls for them in exchange for money, goods and/or cigar business. It is rumoured that these men also like to make videos and it may well be that such amateur pornography is among the contraband they smuggle.

Mark has a very specific sexual preference for young teenagers. He approaches girls who either are, or who look about 13 years old, and asks 'Are you my baby? My baby, si? You're my baby, si?' The 13 and 14 years old who had sex with him told us that he is extremely tight fisted, only paying them $5 or $10 for a night and asking them to do things that they did not want to do. In particular, he likes to 'buy' two girls and command them to have sex with each other.

Over the five nights we observed him, he had no dealings with any prostitute over the age of 15. John likewise has a preference not only for younger girls but for threesomes, 'parties' and so on with under-age prostitutes. John is divorced and speaks with great bitterness about Canadian women's power over men, a 'power' which is evidenced primarily through their legal right to alimony payments. Bruce likes women to be 'ladies'.

He finds it 'unattractive' for a woman to smoke, drink or swear. He is contemptuous of women he defines as 'real' prostitutes and does not consider the Cuban *jiniteras* he fucks to be prostitutes. They are often 'nice girls' from 'good families' who just want some clothes and some fun.

He had a long term relationship with the 26 years old daughter of a Cuban neurosurgeon, for example, who spoke excellent English and was herself a qualified doctor. There was a 20 years age difference between them as well as a massive inequality in terms of economic power. Any 26 years old doctor from a comparable socio-economic background in Canada would probably judge Bruce to be a fairly unremarkable and mediocre man yet he was certain that his Cuban woman 'was *really* in love with' him.

He had even investigated the possibility of marriage and it was this that ended the relationship for, in his words:

It brought everything home to me. It would've cost me $45,000 to get her out of Cuba [the cost of her medical training], plus she would've had to spend another two years in medical school in Canada before she could have practised, plus the Canadian government would make me sign a guarantee that I'd support her financially for ten years. It was just too much. I'm a realist. What if I paid all that and then she found herself some young guy? It was a dead end relationship. They're all dead end relationships. This is a fantasy world, even she called it that, *fantasia*'.

In other words, Bruce did not wish to compete on a level playing pitch. It is a fantasy world because it is so easy for him to forget that it is his economic power and not his personal magnetism which draws women to him.

We did not observe Bruce with any under-age prostitutes but he was unpeturbed by his friends' sexual activities with children and his attitude towards his own illegal practices (smuggling and 'black' market trading) were revealing. He told us that the 'great thing' about Cuba is that because it is a communist country 'everyone is terrified of the authorities'.

What this means is that no matter what a tourist does, he is 'OK.' As Bruce put it, 'No Cuban is going to report a tourist to the police. They know that they'd be in much deeper shit than you'd be'. John and Mark also appear to feel that they live outside the law in Cuba. In fact, the following episode involving Mark suggests that he believes himself to be the law.

One evening, Mark angrily accosted a 13 years old prostitute in a bar and accused her of stealing money from him. She denied it and Mark grew more aggressive, shouting furiously at her and the other women and girls around her 'You're nothing, you're just putas, I'm a tourist'. He threatened to call the police, telling them he could have them all put in prison and demanding that they show him their *carnets* (I.D. cards).

The women and children, all of whom were thoroughly intimidated by him (the 13 years old was crying), were about to produce their carnets to show him when one of the authors (Jacqueline Sanchez Taylor) intervened, saying that he had no right to make such a demand, that he was not a policeman and besides, what had he been, doing with a

13 years old child in his room that she might steal from him in the first place?

This challenge to his authority made Mark shake with fury. He turned on Jacqueline, whom he took to be a Cuban *jiniteras*, shouting 'Who do you think you are? You're nothing, you're nobody' but his Spanish was not fluent enough to deal with the situation. He ended up following her to where the other author was sitting. 'Do you speak English?' he asked, still shaking with rage. 'Then tell her to keep out of other people's business'. Turning back to Jacqueline he said, 'You'd better be very careful. For $20 I can have you hurt badly. For $50, I can have you killed'.

This story reveals a great deal about the way in which such a man can and does imagine himself in Cuba. Mark is a physically nondescript and puny individual, a divorcee in his forties and a less than completely successful estate agent. Back home in Canada, it is he who feels himself to be a 'nobody' and a 'nothing'. In Cuba, by contrast, he fantasises himself to be somewhere between a Rockefeller and a Mafiosi boss.

He believes that his economic power combined with his status as 'tourist' places him above the law and under-age prostitutes told us that he attempts to coerce them into having sex with him and performing for him by threatening to report them to the police for theft if they do not do what he tells them.

The Guilty Widower

This man is a Spaniard, aged 52, a practising Catholic and a fairly successful and bourgeois businessman whose wife died at the beginning of 1995. It was his first trip to Cuba and he had come on a two week package tour of Havana and Varedero with a group of male friends. We met him at the end of his holiday and he clearly felt the need to confess. He had, he told us, been amazed and shocked to find himself relentlessly pursued by women and girls in Varedero. 'It's very difficult for a man. What can you do? They won't leave you alone'. He said that this had all been a new experience for him, that he had never had sex with a black woman before and that the first woman he had picked up in Varedero was: a very dark black woman, very beautiful, how could I resist? But I liked her, I did like her as a person. You have to like a woman as a person, I couldn't get involved in just a cold situation, it has to be romantic. You have to have dinner, be able to talk.

He described all his sexual encounters as a result of 'irresistible temptation' having been placed in his path. He was self piteous about his own situation as a widower, saying how it was easy for the married men to 'resist' temptation. Some of the girls are very young, he told us, only 15 or 16 years old, 'so beautiful' and chasing after him, 'What could I do?' he kept repeating. 'The only way to get rid of them is to push them off and run away.'

So how had he 'got rid' of them after he had sexual intercourse with

You have to give them something. You feel obliged to give money or a gift, otherwise it would be like violence to them. It would be like rape... I bought one girl a bikini... They aren't prostitutes.... Their situation is desperate... I respect women... I treated these girls well, I know their situation is terrible. They have nothing... [Why not just give them money as a gift then?] You have to have sex with them, they feel obliged to do something for you in return.

He had had sex with a 15 years old girl who would not now leave him alone. She wanted to travel to Havana with him to spend the final days of his holiday with him. He did not want her to accompany him. 'The Spanish are too romantic' he told us, 'they end up falling in love and marrying these girls. They take them back to Spain with them and the girls just divorce them a few years later'.

Did he feel guilty about having had sex with an underage girl? 'Very guilty, yes. I'm going to go back home and examine my conscience. I'll go to confession'. Did he think he would ever return to Cuba? 'Perhaps, yes'.

Quebecian Retire

This man is a 68 years old retired civil engineer from Montreal. He takes two trips a year, one to Cuba and one to Venezuela, and has been doing so for the past twelve years. He started visiting Cuba on the advice of a friend who has been taking holidays in Varedero since 1980. He considers Venezuela to be more responsive to tourist's 'needs' than Cuba, which he berated as follows:

Nothing works in the hotels, there's not even hot water all the time. They won't let you take lady friends in the hotels, they try to charge you money.... Everyone is corrupt, the police are corrupt, the hotel security is corrupt, everyone is corrupt... You have to take girls to *casa particulars* and they're dirty, they're filthy, there's no shower for you after you've made love.

This man then went into a long diatribe about Cuban 'whores':

Look at them, they're all whores. They want to rob you, they try to cheat you.... They harass [derangent] you... It's changed here, even in the last few months. They're better off now, these girls, they want everything.

One might be forgiven for wondering why, when he finds the country so displeasing, he returns to visit it year after year. A possible explanation was provided by two 13 years old prostitutes and by Rudolpho (one of our key informants) all of whom were familiar with this man's sexual tastes. He is attracted to very young girls—when 13 years olds are procured for him, he complains that they are too old (this may account for the problems he experiences with hotel security). He likes to take such girls into a room and masturbate as he watches them undress.

Charlie

Charlie is an Italian-Canadian, an unmarried semi-retired cabinet maker aged 54. He was on his fourth visit to Cuba and had visited the Dominican Republic twice as well as taking regular trips to Mexico over the past six years. Like many other sex tourists, he funds his trips to Cuba by smuggling clothing into the country and cigars out of it. He prefers to give clothes to the Cuban women and children with whom he has sexual intercourse rather than paying them in cash, as he has friends in the rag trade in Canada and can get items of clothing for a matter of cents.

He was holidaying this time with a male friend, Nigel, also Italian-Canadian and some ten years his junior. Charlie and Nigel were both regular prostitute-users in Canada and had both used prostitutes while living or travelling in Europe as well as in Latin America.

Charlie told us a story about an 'experience' in Germany (where he lived for some months) from which we infer that he has been prosecuted in the past for the sexual abuse of children. He said that he used to invite girls aged between 11 and 14 into his apartment sometimes and that on one occasion a neighbour had called the police. The girl in question had been interrogated and Charlie was taken in for questioning. He did not say what the outcome was but did say that he is now very careful not to have dealings with underage prostitutes in Europe or North America because it 'isn't worth the trouble'.

Charlie is a man whose attitudes and capacity to dehumanise others is: frightening and the two hours spent listening to him were disturbing. Yet because he wanted to defend his behaviour and was intelligent enough to articulate a rationale for it, he was an extremely useful informant. Charlie openly admits to sexually exploiting children of 12 and 13 years old in Cuba and the Dominican Republic. He justifies this in the first instance through a form of cultural relativism.

In 'Third World countries', Charlie argues, attitudes toward sexuality and childhood are very different from those adopted in the West. An Argentinean friend who lives in the Dominican Republic had once picked up two 13 years old girls and explained to Charlie 'it was OK to fuck them'. No-one cares in the Dominican Republic, the police don't care, the kids' parents don't care, there are no laws against it [sic], because it is seen as natural. Children grow up faster in places like this than they do in industrialised countries.

In Canada, a seven years old has to be looked after by its parents or else it will wreck the house. In non-industrialised countries, seven years old children look after their baby brothers and sisters. They mature more quickly. But it is not only age that carries a different meaning. The meanings that are attached to sexual acts are also culturally relative. 'There are no taboos about sex here', he told us, 'it's a very open, physical culture'.

The next step in his 'logic' is to assert that children who grow up in these 'open' and 'natural' cultures are sexually knowing. Take Cuba as another example, he continued. Two days previously he had been approached by a 12 years old girl. She told him that she had been divorced for two years, that she had been married at ten:

How can you call that a child? All right, she was 12 years old, but she was a lady. She'd been married for two years. There's no law against it here. Her parents agreed to it. She'd been sexually active for two years. She was a lady. Why should I treat her any different?... Why should we impose our moral standards? Who's to say that our moral standards are right and their's are wrong?... When in Rome, do as the Romans, that's what they say isn't it?

Charlie's Spanish was far from fluent and his account of the 12 years old's story is unreliable for that reason alone. Moreover, his understanding of the law in the economically underdeveloped countries he visits is far from accurate, but the real point to note is that although he argues his case through an appeal to moral relativism (why should the west impose its moral standards on the rest of the world?), he is actually committed to western concepts of childhood.

Western thought defines childhood as a period of sexual innocence, and thus for Charlie, any child who has sexual experience ceases to be a child. In fact, he takes this further and believes that any child who so much as appears (through his eyes) to be sexually knowing is not really innocent and therefore not really a child:

Have you seen the kids dance here? Six year olds waggling their behinds, it's really sexual, even two years old, we saw this little kid the other day, two years old and she was moving her hips, you know, dancing with the mother, moving her body so sexual. They mature young, they're sexual from a young age.

Setting up this polar opposition between the 'sexually knowing', 'sexually innocent' child allows Charlie to tell himself that there is no difference between child and adult prostitutes, and that it is therefore no more morally reprehensible for him to exploit a child prostitute than it is for him to exploit an adult woman prostitute. The 13 years old girl in the Dominican Republic and the 12 years old Cuban girl both 'knew exactly what they were doing'.

He argued that it was a nonsense for people to say that children 'innocent' when they are capable of doing evil.

What about the James Bulger case in England, he asked. Two ten years olds planned a murder and carried it out in cold blood, children are just as manipulative and evil as adults so how can anyone say that these girls don't know what they're doing they go out on the streets soliciting?

Take the girl in the Dominican Republic. She and her friend approached him and the Argentinean, they negotiated a price and went back to the apartment with them. The Argentinean took one of the girls into a bedroom and he, Charlie, looked at the other 13 years old. 'She was expecting some and it wasn't a lollipop. So I let her have it'.

Charlie claims that he does not actively seek out young girls. It is the girls who approach him and he does not differentiate on grounds of age (any girl who solicits is, after all, by definition a sexual adult). He repeated over and over again that it is 'opportunity that makes the thief,' and placed prostitution within his more general set of beliefs about prostitutes, namely that these are females who exploit men's weakness. The 12 years old Cuban girl as much as the adult Canadian prostitute consciously takes advantage of men's biological 'urge' for sex.

He told us he 'hates' prostitutes. He has used prostitutes all over the world and he hates European and North American prostitutes in particular:

It's all businesslike. It's by the hour, like a taxi service, like they got the meter running... There's no feeling. If I wanted to fuck a rubber doll, I could buy one and inflate it. Here it's different. They're not professionals. They enjoy sex, it's natural to them... they're affectionate... they're responsive. They even kiss you. A prostitute in Europe will never kiss you. Canada, it's ridiculous. You know, if you go with a prostitute and you don't pay her, you know what? They call it rape. You can be in court on a rape charge.

He likes the powerlessness of prostitutes in Cuba, Mexico and the Dominican Republic. 'Here, they don't even ask for the money. It's up to you'. In Cuba, sometimes he gives the girl her taxi fare home as well as an item of clothing but he enjoys the knowledge that, as he put it, 'if you don't pay a girl here, there's nothing she can do. She's not supposed to be with you anyway. It's just tough'. The non-contractual nature of prostitution in countries like Cuba and Thailand appeals to 'Mr. Average' type sex tourists because it allows them to deny the commercial basis of their sexual encounters and to tell themselves that the girls are not really prostitutes and they themselves are not really clients.

But Charlie is clear that such women and children are prostitutes a despises them for their 'immorality'. 'Who's to blame for prostitution?' he asks, and answers, 'It's the prostitutes, isn't it? If they weren't there, there wouldn't be any prostitution. They create the situation, they make the opportunities and opportunity makes the thief.

Again, he does not distinguish between adult and child prostitute: I don't go looking for little girls. But if a 15 years old or a 12 years old, if she approaches me, if she comes up to me, what am I supposed to do? If I didn't go with her, what would I be?

We pushed him to say where exactly he would draw the line—what if a nine years old approached him, or a seven years old, for example? He not answer this directly but instead kept saying that it was not up to him to draw the line since he does not initiate such encounters but merely responds to 'opportunities'/expectations of him. This was interwoven with reference back to the idea that a sexually knowing child is not a child but a conscious seductress and, most frightening of all, it was in this context that he again of the two years old child dancing 'provocatively'.

If the culture allows it and the parents allow it, and the girl wants it he went on, where is the harm? There is no psychological harm if every one accepts that it is natural and no physical harm done. What is the fuss about? It's hypocrisy. He supported his claim that no physical harm was referring to something he claimed to have read about rape:

It said that if a man uses a condom, after five minutes, just five minutes after a rape. There's no physical evidence that a girl's even been raped. Doctors can't even tell. The female body is designed to take the man's penis, it doesn't do any damage, there's no physical harm.

Charlie's attitudes towards prostitution and sexuality are easier to understand when considered in relation to his more general attitudes to gender. He spoke at length and with enormous bitterness about male disadvantage. Mothers train their daughters and prepare them for sexual and emotional life. They teach girls how to look pretty, how to sit, how to cross their legs, how to attract men and please them.

But they teach their sons none of these things. The boy is 'neglected' and then, all of a sudden, he is expected to be a man, to be in charge, to know how to deal with women. He is suddenly expected to fight in wars, expected 'to fuck whores', expected to be a real man. The mother is even happy if he dies for his country so long as she gets a flag, neatly folded and a letter saying that her son was brave. The mother doesn't care if her son goes out 'and fucks some dirty whore', she just says 'Good, that shows he's a man'.

Boys get no care, they are not allowed to show emotion. They might be hurt but they have to conceal it, they're not allowed to cry. And no-one has told them how to please women. They reach the age of 15 or 16, they have biological urges, they need to find a girlfriend, so they go out and find themselves humiliated and the girl is just laughing. She knows exactly what to do. 'Men are like yo-yos, emotionally they're controlled by women. It's always women who hold the strings'.

Charlie is not difficult to psychoanalyse. His sexuality is pure infantilism. He is consumed with rage against the mother who 'withheld' care and affection front him and obsessed by the idea of being able to command sexual access in order to reverse the various humiliations which he believes he has suffered at women's hands.

Western prostitutes are not fully satisfying to him because, although he can obtain sexual access to them on demand, they are in a position to set limits on what he can and cannot do, to tell him how much to pay. In this sense, 'whores', as much as madonnas, 'hold the strings'. He is humiliated by their control and his masculinity is therefore incompletely asserted through the act of having sexual intercourse them.

With a Cuban prostitute on the other hand, especially a child prostitute, it is quite clearly him in control and he simultaneously becomes 'the real man' that he feels is expected of him and punishes 'authority' for having such an expectation of him. The latter is important, because Charlie is not just driven by rage against those who have withheld care, he is also obsessed by the idea of authority figures betraying and controlling him. He was angry with his mother, with the church, with the state.

He spoke at length about the hypocrisy and corruption of the powers that be. Governments make their laws and try to impose 'moral standards' but do powerful people live by them? No. So why should he?

Charlie's relationship with authority, especially as constituted by the law, is ambiguous. On the one hand, he blames 'authority' for not holding him in check. He sexually abuses children in Cuba and the Dominican Republic because no authority stops him (the child's parents don't care, the police don't care, nobody cares, so why should he?).

He does not sexually abuse children in Europe or North America because the authorities do stop him. It is not up to him to 'draw the line', he is a passive victim of his own biologically programmed 'needs' and must have someone else (a mummy?) to help him control himself.

He furiously resents any attempt to constrain him and interprets 'obedience' to authority as a sign of weakness. When his travelling companion Nigel disagreed with his views on child prostitutes, Charlie viciously and relentlessly attacked him for being 'easily led' and not an 'individual', for getting his ideas from newspapers instead of 'analysing' things for himself.

CONCLUSIONS

The impact of the sexploitation on the lives of Asian women, men and children are obviously physical, emotional and psychological. Led to believe that they are not worth more than $4.00 a day, the victims of sexploitation live their lives with the painful dichotomy of self-sacrifice and degradation. The lack of protection from their Government and their family leaves these people to feel completely and utterly disabled, vulnerable and marginalized. Some even die by this profession.

In 1973 the Women's League of the South Korean Christian Church and the Japanese Asian Women's Association protested against sex tourism (Kim, 192). Even when concerns are voiced, little is changed because of greed. The airlines no longer make the "hospitality women" a main feature but that is a small part of the advertisement of sex. The protests may have eliminated one avenue of the sex industry but others are still engrained in society.

Men profit from the tarnished industry. Businessmen are known to treat their clients to dinner, entertainment, and women. As men recommend a prostitute's services or escort her to a paying customer's room, she must in turn give them a cut of her earnings. The prostitute must further appease hotels and the local Government with monetary bribes.

Physical abuse and the lessened value of women is shown in a 1983 survey that reports 61.2% of Korean men openly admit to beating their wives. Disgraces in law are shown in the standard jail sentence because rape in Thailand sentences a man to three years, while robbery calls for a five-year punishment (Kim, 187). Even when other laws limit the promotional information available to sell adult women for prostitution, another avenue of the sex industry is opened. Children have become the new commodity in Bangkok and Manila.

Young girls in their early teens are turned into sex machines. Their virginity is prized, but after being deflowered the pre-teens are just another streetwalker. The severe impact this has on a young child is deduced to a sacrifice for her family who profits from a daughter working. It is the daughter's obligation to sell herself in honour of Thailand's feudal tradition. The income allows the parents to buy televisions or support the rest of the girl's brothers and sisters. It is sad to think that a "Thai woman can earn two or three times as much in the sex service industry as she can in unskilled industrial or agricultural work (Kim, 188)."

Abolishing sex trafficking can never result to just one quick solution. Instead, the complex issues behind the walls of oppression have to first be considered. Thus, there has to be an attempt at breaching the economic gap between Third World countries and the industrialized power houses in the world. Also, in the same way that "America being the saviour" has been conditioned into the minds of many women, the concept of a woman having value has to also be conditioned into the patriarchal societies that these women live in. Also, the Government has to take part in social change. That means eradicating hypocrisy, providing jobs and turning away the demands for sex work.

6

CHILD SEX TOURISM CAMPAIGNS

No other human rights or environmental campaign has influenced the international tourism industry in the way that the campaign against child sex tourism has done. ECPAT groups have been at the forefront of campaigning and some of the first leaflets and posters ever produced 10 years ago were by PEACE in Sri Lanka and ECPAT Philippines, both still active in campaigning against child sex tourism.

So why does child sex tourism still exist? Does this mean that the international campaigns to prevent child sex tourism have failed to make an impact?

The answer to the last question is clearly no, there has definitely been an impact but how do we evaluate it? More importantly how can we learn from it so that future campaigns can become more successful?

Many ECPAT groups have developed creative campaign actions based on communicating, a message through posters, leaflets, luggage labels, stickers and more recently through TV spots and in-flight videos. Most of these actions have been awareness-raising activities but once we have raised awareness in the community what do we do next? Raising awareness is only one part of the prevention cycle.

Other stages in the cycle include defining the problem through research and consultation, initiatives to reduce the root causes and program evaluation. All of these stages can include the active participation of stakeholders including those most affected.

As ECPAT crows, new partners look toward established campaigns for models that they can replicate. However, within the ECPAT movement we have been slow to analyse the collective impact of our campaign actions using a common set of indicators.

INDICATORS

The most elusive yet most important question is what are we trying to achieve and what indicators can we use to measure it? Of course, we are working toward a higher goal of eliminating commercial sexual exploitation of children—but a leaflet or a poster on it's own won't do that.

If successful campaigning is about achieving a change of behaviour or attitude then a campaign tool such as a leaflet, poster, sticker or in-flight video should have a clearly defined objective and a set of indicators to help measure its effectiveness and contribution to the overall success of the campaign.

The best way to develop indicators for monitoring and evaluation is by being as detailed as possible about the purpose and objective of the campaign tool and then develop a plan according to the specific needs of the audience (target market). The tool will be more successful if you match the right message to the right audience and distribute in the right location segmenting the market.

Some indicators are easily defined but planning is still important. For example, a leaflet that's purpose is to encourage people to report child abuse to a police hotline and it's objective is increased reporting of child sex crimes then one indicator would be the number of phone calls made to the police hotline. But have you planned thoroughly for other variables? Is the hotline open 24 hours? Can people call it from other locations without incurring long distance charges? Do the police service have the capacity to handle a large volume of calls? Will the police service give you statistical data to evaluate? What is the target audience that you want and how will you get the leaflet to them?

Alternatively, if the leaflet is about deterring the potential offender what planning have you done? Why have you made the assumption that an offender will be deterred by reading a leaflet? Have you asked offenders whether they would be deterred if they had seen a leaflet? If so, how will you get your leaflet to places that best targets the potential offender?

Once you have gone through these and other more specific questions it becomes easier to develop indicators for monitoring and evaluation strategies. The first example is straightforward: the number of calls to police. But in the second example the indicators become less clear. Measuring the prevention of a crime is a difficult concept especially when baseline data is not available.

EVALUATION

Evaluation comes in four basic forms—process evaluation, content evaluation, impact evaluation and ethical evaluation. Most of us find it easiest to do process evaluations. For example: we produced 20,000 leaflets at x cost, distributed to y outlets between the months of June to December. Most donor agencies ask for this type of quantifiable evaluation.

However, in order to measure the overall contribution to the campaign we should attempt to follow through with the other three methods, especially impact evaluation. Unfortunately, donor agencies are not always sympathetic to extending funding for these purposes once the activity is completed. Lack of funds is a real barriers to effective planning and evaluation.

Impact evaluation should include a medium to long-term review process through methods such as focus group discussions, stakeholder consultations and surveys for feedback. For example, in the case of the leaflet encouraging people to report child abuse to police what impact has this had on the police as well as on child victims? Were the police adequately trained to handle an increase in the volume of calls? Were there adequate legal and welfare services for children who were rescued as a result of increased calls? Has the increase in calls resulted in increase convictions or additional resources for police and other services protecting children?

With impact evaluation we also must face the possibility that there was no impact or negative impact. This is difficult to report especially when future funds are dependent on a successful outcome. However, by documenting and sharing lessons learned the implementing agency will help others to improve future campaigning activities.

Content evaluation includes things such as 'readability' or clarity of language and style, effectiveness of visual images, appropriate use of multiple languages to cater to different nationalities or ethnic groups. Does it give enough direction to the audience to help them do what they are being asked to do? Focus groups and surveys are a good way to evaluate content.

Ethical evaluation is rarely done but an important reflective tool. One outcome of child sex tourism campaigns has been the tendency for police authorities in some countries to do a 'sweep' of sex workers off the streets. This would be considered an ethical issue and would have to be addressed as part of the overall campaign planning and evaluation.

Child sex tourism is a global phenomenon—it is crime that knows no borders and offenders are using new, often sophis-ticated ways of avoiding detection.

PSYCHODYNAMIC EXPLANATIONS OF CHILD SEXUAL EXPLOITATION BY TOURISTS

To what extent can the sexual exploitation of child prostitutes by the sex tourists we observed and interviewed be explained through reference to individual psychology?

Psychologists sometimes characterise paedophiles as 'narcissists' who conceive of childhood as a period during which individuals are the 'focus of uncritical, maternal admiration' and are attracted not towards a particular child or children but to 'what these children represent as imagined replicas' of themselves as children (see Ennew, 1986: 51).

The men profiled above would not all conform to clinical definitions of 'paedophile' since they are chiefly attracted to post rather than pre-pubertal children. Yet, in the sense that men like Charlie, Mark, Jake and John also seem to be angry with a society that does not concur with their own much inflated view of themselves and more particularly, a society that imposes constraints on them rather than indulging them absolutely, the concept of narcissism is useful in understanding their motivations. Sex tourism satisfies their narcissism by giving them a space within which their own image of themselves is reflected back (they can see themselves as economically, socially and sexually powerful, and it also makes it possible to transcend the rules that constrain them at home and so to flout authority.

The desire to challenge authority and assert control over other people as sexual beings appears to be strongly related to these men's sense of their own masculinity, and the psychoanalyst Robert Stoller's discussion of perversion is enlightening in this respect. Stoller argues that in men:

perversion may be at bottom a gender disorder (that is, a disorder in the development of masculinity and femininity) constructed out of a triad of hostility: *rage* at giving up one's earliest bliss and identification with the mother, *fear* of not succeeding in escaping out of her orbit and a need for *revenge* for her putting one in this predicament (1975: 99).

In word and deed, these men express rage at not being the central focus of an adoring and indulgent gaze, at not being able to *command* a woman's undivided attention and unswerving loyalty. Adult women who are their economic, social and/or legal equals are perceived as hugely threatening not because they actually control men but because they are in a position to control *themselves*, that is to say, to exercise choice over whether or not to meet a man's demands.

It is no good marrying a Cuban woman and taking her back to Canada where she would be in a position to choose to end the relationship. It is no good entering into a long term relationship with a western woman who is in a position to decide whether or not she wants to give you your nightly 'massage'. It is not even any good using a prostitute if she is in a position to determine the limits of the contractual exchange. For a woman to be in position to exercise choice is for her to assert her separateness, her free will, her capacity to freely withdraw from the relationship and thus to arouse these men's infantile rage.

One glimpses both the fear and revenge that Stoller refers to in the dire (hostility expressed by Charlie, and by Mark's shouting 'You're nothing you're just putas!' and by the French Canadian's venom against 'dirty, cheating whores'. But in terms of understanding why such men sexually abuse children, it seems more important to note that this kind of fear could lead to a search for sexual partners who are perceived as too powerless to pose serious threat to their control.

Meanwhile, because having sex with children is transgressive, it represents a form of revenge against the authority figures who try to control them and a world that refuses to gaze indulgently upon them.

We feel, however, that explanations which focus on individual psychology can only partially explain the phenomenon of child sexual exploitation by sex tourists. Some abusers do clearly suffer from what might be readily classifiable as personality disorders—Charlie, Mark and the French Canadian retiree being the most obvious examples.

But others neither exhibit traits nor express attitudes that fall outside what would be generally accepted as 'normal' in North American and European society. Indeed, the only characteristics which interviewees to date have consistently had in common is their racism, their sexism and their adherence to a very specific set of beliefs about male sexuality, none of which could be said to distinguish them from the mass of their male compatriots.

SOME COMMON THEMES

Some common themes emerge from the profiles provided above, as well as from interviews with other sex tourists who were observed with under-age prostitutes.

1. Male Sexuality as Biological 'Need'

All are men who believe themselves to be at the mercy of biologically determined sexual 'needs' or 'urges'. They therefore see women as having control over a 'resource' (their female bodies) which is vital to men's well-being. Western women, who are generally in a position to limit or deny them access to this vital resource, are therefore seen as powerful. Not all these men are equally angry about the imaginary power which women hold over them. There is a big difference between a man like Charlie and one like the Spanish widower in terms of how centrally preoccupied they are by the idea of this 'power', for example. Yet both these men feel it is unreasonable to expect them to resist any 'opportunity' to obtain access to this resource, 'What was I supposed to do?' they both say.

Because all of them buy into a model of male sexuality which is couched in terms of 'needing' rather than 'wanting', they can construct themselves as passive victims of 'nature' rather than as active agents, which in turn means that they do not see themselves as fully morally responsible for their actions.

2. 'Racialised' Others as Sexual Others

All are men who espouse a highly sexualised form of racism. Western thinking on 'race' stills owes much to the pseudo-science of nineteenth century anthropologists and natural scientists who elaborated the idea of a hierarchy of 'races' which was seen as somehow linked to an evolutionary process. Whites, needless to say, were the most highly evolved, whilst so called 'primitive' people were taken to exist 'in a state of nature'.

Without exception, the sex tourists we interviewed reproduced this classic racism in their (mis)understanding of Cuban culture as sexually 'open' and 'free'. Indeed, their racism has an extraordinary self-reinforcing quality, since it encourages them to interpret everything they see as 'evidence' of the truisms they already 'know'.

The fact that young couples sometimes have sex on beaches or in the sea is interpreted as an expression of urgent, primitive animalism rather than as a response to a chronic housing shortage and lack of privacy, for example, and the fact that girls who are unwashed and barefoot approach tourists to prostitute themselves is interpreted as a sign of their 'simplicity' and 'artlessness' (they have come 'straight from the jungle') rather than as a testament to their poverty and desperation,

The sex tourists' racism is gendered—it is Cuban women and girls in particular who are alleged to be so very 'natural' and 'physical'—but it also seems to us that this kind of sexualised-racism may serve to disinhibit sex tourists about adult-child sexual contact in two main ways. First, there are men like Charlie whose racism dehumanises children in the economically underdeveloped countries they visit. This allows such men to construct a fiction within which children want and consent to sexual relations with adult men: under-age Cuban girls are just as 'hot' for it as adult women; they grow up young; they're all 'at it' anyway; no 'civilised' inhibitions temper 'their' physical lusts, and so on.

Second, there are men whose racism naturalises adult-child sexual contact in the economically under-developed countries they visit. Since they believe that all men have a biologically programmed 'natural' urge to seek sex, there must be a sense in which Canadian and European sexual law and morality represent an attempt to restrain 'nature' and is thus 'unnatural'. (A sex tourist once told one of the authors that he had seen Desmond Morris talking on TV and had suddenly understood that 'I'm a walking sex machine' and that this explained his 'need' to go to Thailand.) What Jake an ageing hippie sex tourists like him do is to set up an opposition between the imaginary sexual freedom of the 'noble savage' in Cuba and the restrictive repressive codes and laws governing sexual expression in Canada.

The latter are viewed as an attempt to hold in check what is 'only natural', the former becomes something wholesome, good and 'natural', a palliative against the evils of modernity and materialism. And we all know the 'natural' things are good for children, or at least, that they do children no harm.

With the possible exception of the Spanish widower, the tourists profile above were preoccupied with issues of authority and control. They all railed against bad and corrupt authority figures and saw themselves as somehow above the law (this finds expression in the smuggling activities as well as in their sexual exploitation of under-age prostitutes). Again, this suggests that they view laws pertaining to sexual conduct as illegitimate, presumably believing that state has no right to invade their freedom to satisfy 'natural' wants and appetites.

Respect, the Austrian Center for Tourism and Development, conducted an evaluation of the in-flight video screened on Austrian Airlines on their long haul flight to India and South Africa.

Quantitative data, based on a questionnaire, was complied, and face-to-face interviews by a team of researchers working on the flight provided qualitative data. 87% of the interviews received the video positively, and approved of this type of awareness action in-flight. The majority felt that the tourism industry has not been active enough in terms of passenger education. Prior to the video, nearly 50% of the interviews were unaware of the possibility of prosecution in their home country. Negative reactions, where they occurred, might have been provoked by the fact that the video was screened without preparing (i.e., informing) the passengers of the nature of the content.

The National Commission for Women is an apex body in India created by an Act of Parliament called the National Commission for Women Act, 1990 (No. 20 of 1990). The Act came into force in January, 1992. The Commission consist of a Chairperson, five members and one Member Secretary—all nominated by the Central Government. The main functions of Commission are to investigate and examine all matters related to the safeguards provided for women under the Constitution and other laws; to forward recommendations for the effective implementation of those safeguards for improving the conditions of women by the Union or and State; to take up the cases of violation of the provisions of the Constitution and of other laws relating to women with the appropriate authorities; to look into complaints and take *suo motu* notice of matters relating to either deprivation of women's rights or non-implementation of laws enacted to provide protection to women or non compliance of policy decisions and to take up such matters with appropriate authorities; to call for special studies or investigations into specific problems or situations concerning women and thereby recommend strategies for their removal; to inspect or cause to be inspected a jail, remand home, women's institution or other places of custody where women are kept as prisoners or otherwise, and take up with the concerned authorities for remedial action, if found necessary; to fund litigation involving issues affecting a large body of women.

All the reports to be laid before each House of Parliament along with memorandum explaining the action taken or proposed to be taken on the recommendations. The Commission also has all the powers of a Civil Court trying a suit and in particular in respect of the matters namely—summoning and enforcing the attendance of any person from any part of India and to examine him on oath; requiring the discovery and production of any document; receiving evidence on affidavits; requesting any public record or copy thereof from any court or office to issue to the Commission for the examination of witnesses and documents and any other matter which may be prescribed.

Keeping in mind the fact that commercial exploitation of children and traffic in persons for commercial sex abuse is the worst form of violation of human rights, and the number of children entering the trade is on the increase, sexual exploitation of women and children became a key area of concern for the Commission. In view of it, studies were commissioned in ten States to assess the magnitude of the problem. The findings of the studies revealed a very dismal and horrible position.

In order to focus attention on the problem, the Commission organized conferences, workshops, debates and meetings during 1995. The Chairperson and Members of NCW made a nationwide tour and met more than 80,000 women in prostitution and child prostitutes in different States of India, got acquainted with their problems, evironmental conditions, health status, their requirements and concerns. The Commission held several consultations with NGOs and activists. NCW also sponsored research studies in the States of Orissa, Goa, Andhra Pradesh, Kerala, Karnataka, Rajasthan, Delhi, West Bengal and a part of Madhya Pradesh which includes survey of several brothels and streets in order to get firsthand authentic information regarding the status of child prostitutes.

The studies revealed a dismal position and confirmed the apprehensions of NCW that the network involves not only traffickers but pimps and brothelkeepers also who work in connivance with the police. The recommendations have been sent to the concerned Department of Government of India and all the State Governments for follow up action. The State Governments are taking effective and prompt action on the recommendations of NCW with a view to eliminating the evil. The NGOs are being more actively involved.

The Commission has been resolutely striving to improve the condition of women and usher a new culture by trying to eliminate gender discrimination. In pursuance of its goals, the Commission has constituted several Expert Committees to look into specific issues relating to women and give their recommendation for further action. The NCW had also defined its priorities and thrust areas and has initiated several plans and programmes to implement them. The thrust areas of NCW include; *speedy justice for women* through Parivarik Mahila Lok Adalats, *legal awareness programmes* for Women's Colleges by providing legal training to teachers and students to spread massive legal awareness; *custodial justice*—in coordination with National Human Rights Commission trying to implement support and *rehabilitation measures for women undertrials and prisoners, widows, destitutes and recommend to government for rehabilitating women and children in prostitution* and women in mental asylums, by establishing network with NGOs, State Commissioners for Women, Minorities Commission, Law Commission, University Women's Study Centre, UN and other international agencies and State Coordinators, *anti-arrack campaigns, political empowerment of women,* creating awareness and empowering women of *Scheduled Castes and Scheduled Tribes, Sathins, grass roots workers* and also *economic empowerment* of women through *transfer of technology.*

The NCW has successfully handled critical issues of atrocities on women, e.g., the Uttarkhand, incident outraging modesty of women, sexual harassment at work, dowry harassment and death and gender based denial of opportunities. In order to achieve its goals, I travelled widely all over India, held consultations with women in remote villages and had meetings with women of every section. To create awareness among the public several seminars and meetings had been held from time to time, the proceedings of which are carefully recorded to formulate plans of action. During such visits the plight of women and especially of young girls of a tender age of ten years selling out their bodies for two rupees was observed by me as the Chairperson. They are either pushed into this practice by parents due to poverty or are victims of trafficking.

The Government of India as also most of the State Governments, are aware of the enormity of problem of child prostitution. Under the orders of the apex court of the country a Central Committee under the Department of

Women and Child Development has been formed which is looking into the different aspects of the problem. There is also a proposal to convene a meeting of SAARC countries to finalize SAARC regional convention of combatting trafficking in women and children in the region.

The prevent entry of children in prostitution, NCW has involved the prostitutes themselves to undertake this onerous responsibility. The women themselves came forward and declared that they will be able to prevent it and assured me as Chairperson that entry of children into this profession would be tackled. They were also ready to inform new child entries to the NCW or the State Commissions instead of the police.

Braving the mafia and its criminal nexus the women and children in prostitution offered to undertake this responsibility which is not only laudable but most welcome. The NCW firmly believes that this will be a feasible modality to save children from prostitution. While rehabilitation has to encounter numerous hurdles and handicaps preventive measures are thought of as urgently needed and a practical solution.

Women have come forward to seek adequate shelter for themselves and their children. They also express their willingness to opt out of this demeaning profession if they are provided shelter and a modest income of Rs. 1,000–1,500 per month. I have appreciated the reality of such women who came forward in large numbers to lead a normal life away from exploitation and dishonour. Their immediate need for shelter, skill employment and regular income can no longer be over looked and demand the immediate attention of government and public.

The goal of NCW is to achieve "zero level" child prostitution. To achieve this, the Commission is formulating a ten-year National Plan of Action (1997–2006 A.D.). Split into two parts, the plan would coordinate with the Ninth and Tenth Five-Year Plans of India.

To arrive at the 'priority objective' or zero level, the Commission intends utilizing both positive and negative methodologies Positive methods involve rescue operations and rehabilitation measures for victims already in the profession. Negative measure aim at negating entry to new entrants to the profession. For this the Commission intends to have access to fully develop intelligence network. There have been significant advances in meeting the problem head on over the past three years. Awareness raising and public information campaign on children's issues have been pursued with vigour. There is a strong NGO movement in India. They are in the forefront of the crusade against child about and commercial sexual exploitation. The National Commission for Women recognizes their contribution in responding to the needs of the local and international fronts. Thus, it is imperative that all concerned—the government, NGOS, the media and the community pay more attention to strengthen response mechanism to reorient cultural attitudes and social values to be more sensitive to the child; to increase advocacy for children's right, and to work towards a more active participation of children in all matter affecting their lives.

CASE STUDIES

Nepal

She was merely nine years old, content with her daily work, play and the scolding she frequently received. Her father sold her to the Bombay man" for $14. That man asked her if she would like to go to India's entertainment capital. She remembers thinking: "Bombay is where all the films come from" and excitedly agreed.

Her first stop, though was at Bordello in the northern Indian border town of Gorakhpur, where she was "broken in" as she says. Then Saroj was sent to Pila House, one of Mumbai most decadent brothels. She was put in a small room with a tiny window that had iron bars on it. On one wall there was a calender that had a picture of the mountains and she was reminded of her house with mountains.

For fifteen days she was beaten and whipped until she agreed to service clients. At 3 p.m. everyday she was forced to put on make-up and wait. On average she serviced six men a day for Rs. 60($1.60) a session. She never saw any money for five years, until her employer's investment was paid off. Saroj says she was constantly ill but could only visit a local medical quack with an escort for 10 minutes at a time.

Now seventeen and a bonded prostitute, she lines the dim, beaten stained corridors of Pila House night after night along with other girls, their faces easily beautiful as though airbrushed for a pornographic, magazine. "I send my family in Nepal Rs. 1000[$27] per month," she says. "Sometimes I also send them video cassettes of myself with messages. We have a lot of countrymen who charge a small sum to take money and messages to my family. "Saroj has not been back to her village near Kathmandu since she left nor does she plan to return." "What will I do there?" is her query.

Mumbai has been given her a two-year old son, and tuberculosis! and has also tested HIV positive! "I dont't care if I die but I would like my son grow up somewhere else" she says wistfully. The toddler sleeps under her bed while she services clients. Does she insist on condoms? "No. If I talk about condoms, the client wants to know if I have a disease. I have no bargaining power." The Gharwali (brothelkeeper) has promised her a ticket home if she gets worse. "I will just be a liability and of no use to anyone if my body deteriorates" she says matter-of-factly.

A visit to Saroj's village in the Sindhupalchowk district of Nepal on a hot afternoon showed that her house was one of the few with a corrugated-tin roof and a radio. Her brother was playing cards at a nearby tea shop and her father was sleeping. Her mother was working on someone else's field. Saroj's brother and those hanging out with him were resentful of questions. "What is the harm?" he asks, referring to his sister working as a prostitute in Mumbai. "At least she can contribute to her family. Our neighbour's daughter has just come back [from India] after 18 years. She has brought back Rs. 25,000 ($680) cash and 12 tolas (140g) of gold."— Brother's love and father's greed. Nepal has become one of the most accessible areas for sex traffickers working in South and West Asia.

Reema

She was barely twelve when a smooth-talking flesh trader lured her to Mumbai from Kathmandu. The starry-eyed girl wanted to become a film actress. Instead, she was sold to a brothel. At first see resisted—screaming, crying and attacking all prospective customers. But the madam who ran the brothel would have none of it. She sent in a muscled tough to pin the girl down while an old man deflowered her. The pain was so intense that Reema lost consciousness and had to be hospitalised for a week. After that it was back to the brothel.

But Reema's spirit was not broken. Nine months later she escaped from the brothel and got into a Howrah-bound train, hoping to eventually reach her home in Nepal. At Howrah, a soft-spoken lady promised to help; she lured the young girl to a Calcutta brothel and sold her. Reema had only managed to escape from one brothel to another.

Now, Reema appears resigned to her fate. She hits the streets of central Calcutta as soon as it gets dark and stands under a lamp-post soliciting customers. Her parents in Nepal have no idea where their daughter is. Shee does not have the courage to tell them the truth and cannot make herself lie; and anyway, they probably think that she is dead and it is better that way, she insists. But she still dreams of making enough money to escape to a life of freedom and dignity.

Mira

Mira was thirteen years old when a man from Mumbai came to her remote village in Nepal looking for a domestic servant. He was offering 600 rupees a month, a fortune to subsistence farmers scratching out a living, Mira wanted to go. Not only had Mira never gone to school but she had never ventured beyond her village. She imagined Mumbai would be magical place filled with Hindi movie stars. She knew that if she stayed at home she would become a burden to her father who couldn't afford to pay the dowry for her marriage.

Mira was bundled off in a produce which took her to Mumbai. She quickly realised she would not be working as a domestic servant at all. She was delivered to a brothel in the notorious Falkland Road, where tens of thousand of women and girls are displayed in row after row of cages. Mira was locked into a narrow windowless room without food or water. On the fourth day, when she still refused to work, one of the brothel owner's thugs banged her head against the concrete floor until she passed out.

She was never allowed to leave the red-light area and, in any case, where would she go ? In Mira's case, her freedom from the brothel was purchased by a client who became her pimp. Today, at the age of 35, no longer prostitute, she runs a small tea shop in Mumbai. (Extract from "India's Shame," published by *The Nation*, 8th April, 1996).

Delhi

Urmila is tall, lean and dark in complexion and 15 years old. She lost her father at the age of ten; she has two younger sisters. Her mother is running charcoal business and her monthly income is only Rs. 150/- within this meagre income she has to run the family. At the age of 12 she was fond of seeing cinemas; but she was not permitted to see any films by her mother. One day for the first time she went to see a movie evening show (6 p.m. to 9.30 p.m.) without informing her mother. She was afraid that her mother would beat her severely for late coming, so she wanted to stay outside. She saw some young girls sleeping on the door steps of the shops in the vegetable market; she also slept along with other girls. The next morning, she could see the young girls selling vegetables and making money; so the also started selling vegetables. She could see more and more films with the money she earned. Besides, it was an added income to the family; her mother also encouraged her mean while she could see some of her friends spending money lavishly. She learnt that other vegetable vendors used to have illicit relationship with rickshawalas who bring vegetables to the shops. Soon Urmila was also in the trap. When her mother knew what the girl was up to she chained and kept her in the house. One day, she ran away and landed up in a brothel.

Tamil Nadu

Fifteen-year old Radha is short statured and looks neither attractive nor ugly. Her father is a mat seller at Tiruchendur and was earning sufficient income. He was having a concubine and lived with her. Her mother had deserted him because of his ill-treatment. Owing to the ill-treatment of the stepmother, Radha was ten years old, she came to the bus stand and started begging to get some cash for travel. Meanwhile, she came across an old lady, who took her to a house where there were seven young girls who smoked, drank and played cards. It was a brothel. She was forced into prostitution. So she ran away and came to her father's house. After some days father, step-mother and brother came to know about her stay at the brothel and drove her away from the house. So she was left in the streets. Meanwhile, Radha passed from girlhood to womanhood. She planned to visit her aunt's house at Tirunelveli. While she was begging at the bus stand, she met a teenaged girl who took her to another brothel.

Rosa

Rosa is an eighteen-year old mother. She is short, fat and wheat yellowish in complexion. She hails from Thalaikulam village of Kanyakumari district. Her father, a radio mechanic earns a measly income of one hundred rupees. Her mother is casual coolie and her income is uncertain on most days. Rosa is the second child to her parents, her elder brother is an agricultural labourer and the younger two sisters are studying in seventh and fifth standards respectively. She went to school up to the fourth standard and thereafter she was make to look after household affairs. She was given in marriage, to a jobless man, who went to Thiruvanantha puram in search of a job. He never returned and thus she was deserted. Meanwhile she delivered a male baby too. She felt that both her child and herself are incumbent on her parents. Often she ran into conflict with her parents over financial matters. One day her son became sick and she wanted to take him to the Government Hospital at Kottar, Nagarcoil, so she sought the help of her mother for the bus fare and other expenses. Her mother refused to give the money, instead told her to give the child locally available native medicine. But she borrowed money from the neighbours and came to the hospital. After taking the treatment for her son, she was not having money to go to Thalaikulam. At the hospital she met one middle-aged lady, who told her that she would offer her a job and took her to a house located in Kulamankaran in Nagarcoil (otherwise known as the red-light area of Nagarcoil). She found there were young girls making money through the flesh trade. As the was deserted by her husband, and left with no means of subsistence, she volunteered to enter into this easy profession to maintain her livelihood.

Rajammal

Rajammal is a beautiful, tall and fair complexioned girl with lovely long hair. She belongs to Narasinganallur village in Tirunelveli district. She is seventeen years old. Her father is a physically handicapped person and can't walk properly. He is running a petty shop. The mother is a beedi worker. She is the eldest child to her parents; other youngsters are three brothers and four sisters. She often went to the cinema without the permission of her parents and was an uncontrollable child. She developed friendship with a rickshawala at the age of sixteen. Both loved each other. This news reached the ears of her parents; they often used to beat her whenever she went outside the house without permission. One day her lover took her to cinema for the evening show. After seeing the cinema he told her to come along with him to Tuticorin, where they can get married and settle. Believing all these sweet words, she went along with him to Tuticorin. At Tuticorin, both were staying in a house known to her lover. A few days later he told her that he was going to Tirunelveli and he would return back within two days. But he never returned. Later, she came to know that the house lady was a brothelkeeper and that she had been sold for Rs. 500. In this manner she was forced into prostitution. She refused and ran away to Tirunelveli in sear of her husband. She could not trace him out in the big city. She was wandering here and there to the bus stand; meanwhile she was caught by the police under suspicion and was kept in the police custody. She was released on bail with the help of an old lady. Thereafter she was engaged in beedi making in the old lady's house. Unfortunately one day, the policeman who caught her the previous time came that side. As he wanted a case for that day, without any reason he caught her and charged her. She was again released after a few days. These situations frustrated her and she went again voluntarily to the brothel house at Tuticorin.

Susheela

Susheela hails from Madhuranthangam and is fifteen years old. She had studied till 9th class, but does not have any skills that will find her a job. She was forced to agree to marry a man much older than her. Three days later she came of age, and decided to leave home before the wedding with the help of a young man who worked in the local tea shop. After her arrival in Chennai she lived with this young man for four months. Then he left her with no money, clothes, shelter or food. Although she had an aunt in Chennai she did not wish to contact her because she would send her back to the village.

While wandering around the city she met up with a brothelowner who took her home. Later she was asked to get dressed and entertain men. She later got used to it. Since then she had been sold twice to different brothels. She finally escaped and attempted to make a living by selling flowers and fruits with the help of some friends. This had been difficult as she had no capital. She still has no shelter and sleeps on railway stations or platforms. Hunger continues to drive her to prostitution. She wishes to have at least a place to sleep.

West Bengal

Fourteen-year old Sadhna lived in a village of central Bengal and dreamt of visiting Shantiniketan and Calcutta.

A friend offered to take her to these places. But instead of a pilgrimage to Rabindranath Tagore's abode of peace Sadhna was taken to Sonagachi, Calcutta's biggest red-light area where about 50,000 prostitutes live. There, she was brutally raped and told she would be killed if she did not entertain customers. She did not have the courage to fight back. Then onwards, hers has been a dark world.

Three years have passed since then, Now Sadhna considers herself lucky if she gets customers who pay her not sex —which she hates but just to talk. They pay Rs. 30/- just to sit beside her, and perhaps hold her hands. Last fortnight, she got one such customer. She told him that she likes Hindi songs and has recently acquired a tape recorder. She drinks often as it helps her forget her troubles temporarily.

She hears that her customer has come to Sonagachi in a blue Maruti and wants to go for a ride. The customer, who discovers that Sadhna has never seen any part of Calcutta except Sonagachi, agrees. As the car speeds through Calcutta, Sadhna is transported into another world. She exclaims that it is the best day of her life.

But when the car turns back towards Sonagachi, Sadhna is saddened and retreats into silence. By the time the car enters the filthy lanes of the red-light area, tears glimmer in her eyes. Still, she steadies herself and with a plastic smile, bids her customer good bye. Sadhna knows there is no escape from her sordid world.

Shova Sasmal

Shova Sasmal is nineteen years old and comes from a very poor family. She was forced into prostitution by a relative rather a neighbour. She was sold into a Mumbai brothel and worked for about three years there. She was rescued by the police in 1995 and was kept in Liluah Home.

Sanlaap appealed for her custody. Soon she was sent to Sanlaap shelter and was living with 22 other children. When it was found out that Shova is also HIV positive, counselling and motivation programmes were taken up. She is a brave girl who accepted her sickness with a smiling face.

The village chief and other villagers have decided to pay her a small amount (Rs. 15000/-) from the woman who took her to Calcutta, and the woman has agreed to give it. This trafficker woman has told us that she only trafficked Shova to Calcutta and another man took her to a Mumbai brothel. The name of this man is Gopal Singh and he works at Fairlie Place (Railway) in the personal department. Sanlaap with the help of Panchayat Pradhan could have turned this woman to the police—and gone to the court but there is no substantial or concrete evidence as proof. The trafficker will invariably be out on bail before long and the case can go on for twenty years. By that time Shova might even succumb to death of AIDS.

Andhra Pradesh

Kamala is thirty-two years old, born in Dommari caste and lives in Tadepalligudem. Dommari is a caste which practises prostitution as a caste profession. Kamala grew up as a child with lots of play and the freedom of a child. She never went to school. She was unaware of her mother's profession. She attained puberty at the age of ten years. Thereafter her mother curbed her movements of play and started dressing her like a woman. She was exhibited often to strange men. Whenever she come across strange men in her house she used to be terribly scared. She knows her neighbour, a young man who used to behave intimately with her. She trusted him as a brother. She used to share with him her for of strange men and her mother's strong control. He became very intimate to her and assured that she will be liberated by him from her house. He promised to marry her and live with her. He lured her with number of promises. One night Kamala left her house along with him. Both of them reached Machalipatnam the next morning. After one day's stay and visit to the movies at Machalipatnam he brought her to Tirupati saying that he was going to marry her there. There, she was shocked to see the other side of his face. Suddenly, he became aggressive, threatened her with abusive language and assaulted her sexually. Even before she could recover from the shock, she was already sold for Rs. 5000/- to another person. He took her by force and confined her to a hut in the slums of Tirupati and made her starve. She tried to escape but failed because of vigilant pimps. Her escape bid resulted in further torture and injuries being inflated upon her. The neighbourly women and an elderly women comforted her but slowly initiated her into prostitution. She lived under the iron hand of the man and submitted herself every night to more than eight men. She had to also submit herself to frequent visitors even during daytime. She became mechanical in habit and just survived on the meagre food given to her. After about three years of her pitiable life another man purchased her and took her to Vijayawada. She remained a prostitute for four years in Vijayawada slums. Ultimately she got infected by STD. She fell sick often, but could not discontinue her profession. She hardly had money for treatment. Even the tips she received sometimes from the clients were collected back by the "Aunty". Unable to bear the torture and suffering she was initiated into consuming country liquor.

One morning a party of three men came to her and asked her to follow. She understood that she was further sold again. She was shifted to Chilakaluripet and asked to entertain truck drivers, cleaners and drunkards. The clients used to not only abuse her sexually but sadistically torture her physically, until she became used to it. Until then the clients were brought into her hut/house. But in Chilakaluripet she was asked to stand at the National Highway to attract customers. That is how the responsibility of bringing customers fell on her. She spent another years at Chilakaluripet where she was not even fed properly. Her health had deteriorated vastly. Twice she had to undergo abortions; she underwent surgery. Ultimately one day the strong man asked her to get out of the place as she was no more useful, although she was only 32 years of age.

In search of her parents she reached Tadepalligudem and found that her parents had expired. Currently, she doesn't have a home. Her caste people recognized her and gave her a shelter. But she has no alternative for livelihood. She stands at the roadway of Tadepalligudem and solicits customers on account starvation. She is affected with many ailments and lead a life of orphan. Her income is also meagre. Yet she shares it with others. She is a completely broken women with no future and no hope on her face. She behaves mechanically, often becoming silent on account of her misfortune and suffering.

Kalavati

Kalavati is twenty-one years old and born to Janamma. She doesn't know her father's name. She has a sister. She belongs to 'bogam' caste (dancing girls). Their profession is dancing during the marriages and festivals though she never danced. Her mother used to dance and also continues the profession of prostitution. She takes good care of her two daughters who are her hopes in continuing the business. Kalavati is an attractive girl who attained puberty at the age of twelve. Attracted to her personality a Marwadi middle-aged man paid Rs. 75,000 in installments and took her to Mumbai and kept her as his mistress. She was kept in an apartment in Mumbai. Besides the Marwadi person she was also introduced to three-four other men and coaxed to satisfy them. While she lived as the mistress of the Marwadi man, he encouraged her to earn some more money by providing sex service to a select few brought by him. She was in Mumbai for four years. The Marwadi man brought her back home and left her with her mother.

The Marwadi is a businessman and visits her once a month. Her mother has now stopped the profession and maintains Kalavati and her sister in the profession but for only selected clients. Kalavati is a careful girl, she owns a house and demonstrates the Mumbai life style. Therefore, she is in great demand but she is very choosy. She told us that she is very happy and doesn't want to leave the profession. Kalavati is the rare example being well-off in the profession but still such people are there.

Goa

Manjula, is a young nine year old minor girl lived with her maternal uncle and aunt in Caraswado Mapusa. She would come every morning around 9 a.m. to sell plastic bags. In the afternoon she would spend some time in the open school. After that she would continue selling plastic bags till about 7 p.m.

Manjula would be very badly dressed and did not possess even a pair of slippers. She would earn only Rs. 30/- per day and this would be given to her uncle. She would eat only one frugal meal in the morning; the rest of the day she would survive on cheap snacks available in the market. After a period of nine months, Manjula was seen sporting a smart hair cut started and dressed well, which seemed odd. Her teacher in the open school questioned her and found out that she had about Rs. 300 in her possession.

When Manjula was questioned about it, she told that she was helping somebody to vend articles on Calangute beach. Her mannerisms had changed and she became very cautious about what she spoke. She had around Rs. 500 that day too. From that day she stopped coming to the open school. She refused to talk to the teacher and interact with the other children.

Later she was seen on the beach and her behaviour was alarming. Manjula was not the spontaneous child known for past nine months. She was very uneasy and rude due to the intrusion by others into aspects of her private hidden life. She spoke a smattering of broken English and spoke with an air of false maturity. She said she felt sick and did not like eating although her periods had not yet started so she was afraid though whatever was meant by that was not comprehensible. Manjula did not want to speak to anyone in private. She sent a message that she could not come to school as she was leaving for Bijapur district.

Tanu

Tanu hailed from a well-off family in Bijapur in Karnataka and has studied up to class VII in Kannada medium in her village school. Her maternal uncle was the secretary of the Village Panchayat and held the respect of the whole village. He used to often send the Panchayat peon Sangappa to do petty errands at Tanu's house and before anybody knew what was happening Tanu eloped with Sangappa who brought her to Vasco-da-Gama in Goa, rented a house at Mangor Hill and told her that they will get married once he gets a job. Eight days later Sangappa went out in search of a job and never returned home. Tanu waited for two days before approaching a neighbour. She did not have any money, nor did not know the local language and did not know anybody. She was just thirteen years old then and was very scared. Her neighbours who were also from Karnataka refused to help her. Only the family who rented her the room being local fisherfolk asked her to work in the house to repay their rent. The lady of the house gave her leftover food and asked her to do all the housework. Trouble started two days later, when late in the night the lady's husband forced himself upon Tanu. He told her he would kill her if she told anybody about it. This continued for a week till she dreaded the approaching nights. One night she just walked out on the road and got lost. A man casually spoke to her in her own language and asked for her service for money which she agreed. Two days later she was with Jhansi amma—her gharwali. After a fortnight the red-light area was raided and Tanu found herself in jail.

Malti, Soni, Durga

The first three girls were all fifteen years old. Malti, Soni and Durga, (names withheld) all came from Andhra Pradesh from the village of Hospet. Malti and Durga come from very poor families whose parents are farmers. Their gharwali Jhansi who hails from their native place in Andhra Pradesh is a respected woman in her hometown who boasts that she has "Business in Goa". She requested Malti's and Durga's parents to allow her to take them to Goa to work as housemaids, clothes, food, plus payment would be made. They would be happy and the family would have one mouth less to feed. Their families were given Rs. 2000 each with a promise to send Rs. 500 every month which was two years back. Little did Durga and Malti know what was in store for them.

For the first three days they were kept locked inside a room and were only let out for ablutions and to eat food. When they asked for work the other girls in the room first laughed at them saying they would get plenty of work. After exactly five days "Jhansi Mausi" came in with two men. "We were asked her to go with the men in a Maruti car. We asked her where to go, she said don't get scared, these men will take you to work, see that you work nicely, you must make people happy then only they pay us". Malti recalls how scared she was, Durga and she both clutching each other's hands in fright, and had a premonition something bad was going to happen but they did not know what. The white Maruti car had a driver, one man sat in front and one at the back with Malti and Durga. They don't recall how long they travelled because the whole way they were pawed and pressed by the man sitting with them. Malti and Durga knew no other language other then Telugu and were at a loss what the men were talking but by their lewd behaviour and gestures they were both terribly frightened.

They related that they were taken to a hotel where they were handed over by these men to the "Sahib" waiting in the room. Durga was taken to another "Sahib". They were made to do the most prevent acts by these men but Malti says her "Sahib" was much better. After they came back the hapless girls enquired from each other how much it pained and how many times the "Sahib" asked them to do the horrible acts "sign language". They stayed in the room for nearly six hours. That is what Malti says but Durga says that it was more. Ultimately, they were sent back because Durga was bleeding profusely.

When she was brought back on seeing her condition Jhansi Mausi was furious with the men and took money from them. Durga was taken to the hospital where she was examined by a doctor who gave her in injection and medicines, which the gharwali gave her regularly. In spite of their refusals Jhansi Mausi who told them to call her "Amma" coaxed them to go with men. Says Malti "we were once taken on the ship, and were so scared. We stayed with the phirangis (foreigners) the whole night. I don't know how many times we were forced to do it" and there were so many "phirangis" in the morning we could not even move our legs. But the phirangis gave a watch to Durga. She forgot gave us lots of things. One even gave a watch to Durga. She forgot her pain in the excitement of getting so many things—that also "Phoren". "Now we are used to it. Amma gives us good food and we are able to send around Rs. 2000 home to our family every month".

They do not want to get married and settle down. "Yes, after another two years I will go back to my village and get married but if I have daughter I will never send her to work with any mausi". That was the deep sighed cry of both Malti and Durga.

Karnataka

Lakshmi's grandmother was professional person in prostitution in an area where several generations of women have been involved in this activity. Though her mother was not involved in prostitution she became involved. She had been to school till the 5th standard. Due to economical problems at home her grandmother introduced her to the profession. She had seven siblings. She had liking for this kind of earning. She had great difficulty when she initially started work. The first day was torture. She spent most of the time crying. She protested to her grandmother several times and offered to do house work but she did not listen.

There are increasing police raids nowadays and to pay fines, she had to see many more customers. It is a vicious cycle. If the police leave her alone, may be she can save some money and then try doing something else. But right now she had no solution to her problems.

Kerala

Ramla belonged to a middle class Muslim family in the village of Kumdungal. She is the daughter of an Arabi. She has her mother and three brothers. One brother is employed in the Middle East. Her Bappa used to visit them once in two years. She could study up to VI standard, but does not know writing and reading. She cherishes her childhood memories. Bappa was very affectionate. All the members in the family had concern for her and loved her. At the age of 15, she fell in love with Rashid a man living in the neighbourhood. On the assurance of marriage from Rashid, she left home with him. Rashid brought her to Bangladesh colony. She did not know that Rashid was an alcoholic and a drug addict. Rashid could not live without drugs. When there was shortage of money Rashid began to disturb her, even physically. She had to share her bed with strangers brought by her husband, Rashid. She had no other way but to obey Rashid.

Now she goes to work on her own. She goes to the town on almost all days. Her customers are mostly business people from lodges in this town. She earns about Rs. 300 a day. Occasionally, the police arrest her and lock her up in jail for a few days.

One day Rashid disappeared suddenly. She did not get any information about him for quite a long period. Now Ramla stays with an autorickshaw driver. She has two children from this relationship. He too exploited her and made money from her work. He also deserted Ramla and married another women. Ramla continues to do the same work even today.

Orissa

Sandhya, a resident of Paradeep is in a lucrative profession. She has been providing sexual services since she was fourteen years only. Her base of operation is with her mother who is a commercial sex worker. She pimps for sexual services with the assistance of three Dalals/agents named Ramu, Raju and Kaka. At fourteen she has not reached puberty and yet has been a prostitute in Paradeep for two years. She entertains at least 4/5 clients per day, though she gets lot of offers per day as she is a child prostitute. She earns Rs. 300 per day. She spent 50 percent of her earning on food and clothes.

She has an interest to marry a boy who will love her and protect her. She is not ready to leave the profession unless she is given food and shelter and marriage partner. Her health status is not so good as she does not sleep day and night. She does not use condom as condom is not allowed by the clients.

WHO CARES ABOUT HUMAN RIGHTS ISSUES

There are no real advocates for children. There is no community outrage when children are sleeping on the floor, under sinks and toilets on that kids are locked up with no staff or kids are abducted, sold and abused; there is no outcry

Pandit Jawahalal Nehru was asked by Andre' Malraux: "What has been your greatest difficulty since Independence?" and Pandit Nehru answered "Creating a just society by just means".

Indeed there are few societies which have not faced this difficulty. There has been a widely shared realisation that injecting a bill of rights into a constitution with conventional modes of judicial enforcement for some of the rights is simply not enough. The felt need to fill these glaring gaps acquired urgency as a result of shocking reports of gross human rights violations which went unrepressed, such as torture and rape in police custody, custodial deaths and disappearances, ethnic and communal violence, the revival of slavery in the form of trafficking in women and bonded labour, and pervasive gender discrimination and sexual harassment.

What is Meant by Human Rights ?

Human rights are those rights which are basic to human survival. They are rights and obligations which flow out of our human needs. They are sometimes called fundamental rights, because they are the foundations of our humanity and must be protected.

Human rights as an expression may have a modernising way but as a concern it is as ancient as Plato and Aristotle when "humanity" literally started gaining grounds. Scholars like them taught the then rules that people weren't subjects who are exclusively made to bow but also were "human beings" who needed to be looked after—both physically and emotionally. Leaping into modern times, there is a distant possibility that the study of human rights will become the most genuine interdisciplinary study as it deals with humanity itself. On the practical side of it, a large number of human rights organisations have now been established all over the world to watch and protect right violation.

The human rights of women and of the girl child are an inalienable, integral and indivisible part of universal human rights. Women's place in every community is vital to the well-being of that society; for, without their work, both in the formal sector and in the family, most communities would not survive. It is now well recognised that enhancing women's status and enforcing their rights on an equal basis with men will do much to achieve the objectives of equality, development and peace adopted at the Fourth World Conference on Women held in Beijing in September, 1995 so essential for safeguarding human rights.

The progress of a nation is integrally linked with advancement of women. Mahatma Gandhi championed the cause of women and emphasised that "subjugation and exploitation of women was a product of men's teaching and women's acceptance". We have no dearth of laws. However, implementation of those laws are far from satisfactory. Hence when we talk about gender equity, children's rights and abuse of children, we will have to build up strategies of community participation to checkmate the evil forces all around.

Human rights abuses are wrong in themselves but they also fuel conflict-violence and hatred which result in undermining issues of justice, equity and equality before law.

Women in prostitution face systemic and entrenched discrimination and harassment in term of violence. Child prostitutes are denied access to schools, hospitals, and other public services. They face police brutality all the time and the persistent use of excessive force violates human rights totally. The problem of police abuse in brothels is not a new phenomenon. Today the problem of police abuse is one of the most pressing civil liberties issues. Durga from Bangalore recounted with tears in her eyes, how the police would come with eight to ten men and she was threatened with dire consequences, if she would not oblige. In the beginning when she resisted their demands the police would put red chilli powder in her vagina and torture her with electric shock. Unable to bear she had to succumb to their brutalities.

There are innumerable examples from all over the country of police raids, their undue demands for money, their attacks and their close links with the pimps.

The police often do not even write the reports and justify their rejection to file FIRs by suggesting that the complaints are fabricated. They also deny to file FIRs till such time they are paid and often suggest to these women that their complaints are frivolous and groundless. Sometimes the police say "that all over there are bigger tragedies that are happening, so what is the big issue if a child is molested or raped?". In another case where an eighteen-year-old gild who was molested and raped and beaten for three hours was asked by the police officer. "Why are you so upset, you have not lost your virginity?" Women hesitate to go to the police because it is a frustrating feeling to be treated like that. Sometimes women are called several times to the police stations and harassed. These interviews are generally several hours long and conducted with little regard for the trauma experienced by the victims. A fifteen-year-old victim of gang rape from Chennai told us that she had told her story to police officials at least twenty times. Another young woman who had been raped in Hyderabad, posed with exasperation, "I am tired of telling my story to everyone. I have told it at least ten or eleven times". Although the repeated questioning may be attributable to a lack of police training on how to conduct investigations into sexual violence, the effect of this relentless process is that many victims become intimidated and dissuaded from pursuing their complaints. According to a children's gynecologist in Calcutta, almost all her clients who have experienced sexual violence refuse to go to the police because they are afraid of the questioning and investigation procedures: "It is very difficult for them to go through, all these procedures and all these interrogations. It is a tragedy."

Human rights violations take place due to police excesses on the children in prostitution. Effective and impartial policing is one of the most central components of human rights. During my various visits to the red-light areas I looked around

(1) whether there was any need for change at all in the system;

(2) how could the force become more representative;

(3) whether mechanisms for accountability are sufficient; and

(4) how could police take on a more normal policing attitude and function.

It was generally felt that a change in the system is definitely required as the police force is largely a male dominated institution. We should be recruiting more women and retaining them, and the male the dominated working environment has to be gradually changed. Of course, women within policing crganisations face all the usual problem of working women, and also have the increased stress of working within what is essentially male dominated institution.

However, the presence of more women in the police force would certainly improve the conditions for women in prostitution particularly in a segregated society, and one where the legitimacy of policing is challenged. In this regard thought should be given to the few essential aspects mentioned below :

Training : Having tried to secure a representative body of officers, how do we ensure that their training inculcates in them the important principles of adherence to the basic norms human rights, equality impartiality, and service ? In any democracy, it is vital to ensure that the police generally, as well as individual police officers, are accountable for their actions to the whole of society.

Legal accountability : What legal mechanisms for accountability are required to ensure that the police provide a proper service to the whole community without fear or favour are to be identified and laid down.

Democratic accountability : What are the mechanisms by which society can play in active role in designing and monitoring the kind of police service it wants?

Structure : What should we be looking for in any proposals regarding the structure of policing?

Transition : The above changes, if they are to occur, are dependent on those responsible consciously determining to leave behind the legacy of the past and to bring about fundamental change.

TRAINING IN HUMAN RIGHTS AND ETHICS

Few police forces in democratic societies fail to address issues of human rights in their formal training programmes.

This is only proper since a fundamental objective of policing is to protect and defend the rights of all, to ensure equality before the law, and to do this by having as a primary goal the maintenance of the rule of law.

Community involvement in police training is not, however, a one-way process. It requires not only that the police be open to external involvement and scrutiny, but also requires the ready cooperation of the community. When, for whatever reason, there is distrust or suspicion between the police and parts of the community served, such cooperation may be difficult to establish.

Accordingly, it is not merely desirable for people to discuss and criticise policing—it is a civic responsibility to monitor closely how policing is carried out, and to ensure that it is discharged in accordance with established principles. Policing cannot be viewed in a vacuum. Policing is not only about how individual officers respond to pressure on the streets but it is about a whole array of factors.

It is impossible for even the best police service to please all the people all the time. The role of the police is to manage conflict in the interests of society as a whole. The police must act as neutral arbiters between opposing sides. By acting fairly and impartially they can hope to win support for their right to police.

As Lord Scarman has argued: "The success of policing operations depends in the last resort not upon questions of technique or professional expertise, but upon the degree of confidence felt by society in its police".

We should strongly condemn law and official policies and practices that fail to distinguish between prostitutes and victims of forced trafficking, treating the latter as criminals rather than as persons who deserve "temporary care and maintenance" in accordance with international human rights standards. I strongly oppose laws and policies that punish women who engage in prostitution but not the men who operate and profit from prostitution rings and who patronize prostitutes: such policies are discriminatory on the basis of sex. Moreover, it is of great concern that effective law enforcement and social services for the victims are absent. Such attitudes towards prostitutes exacerbates the problem of trafficking.

INTERNATIONAL LEGAL PROTECTION

Trafficking in persons and related abuses are prohibited under international human rights law. Governments are specifically obligated to take appropriate steps to eradicate forced trafficking in persons, exploitation for prostitution, slavery-like practices, forced labour, and coerced marriage.

TRAFFICKING AND FORCED PROSTITUTION

From the beginning, efforts to create human rights norms regarding trafficking have, in principle, focused on punishing traffickers rather than the victims. International human rights instruments that prohibit trafficking and exploitation of prostitution address these practices in broad terms. It is of particular concern that many state parties have failed to protect women and girls from coerced trafficking and forced prostitution, or have failed to prosecute vigorously those who commit such abuse.

The international community first denounced trafficking in persons in the 1949 Convention on the Suppression of Traffic in Persons and the Exploitation of the Prostitution of Others (the Trafficking Convention). Under the terms of this treaty, state parties "agree to punish any person who, to gratify the passions of another, procures, entices or leads away, for purposes of prostitution, another person." In addition, the Trafficking Convention requires state parties to sanction any person who runs or finances a brothel; in our view, law enforcement agencies should focus particularly on individuals who operate, aid or abet forced prostitution operations. States should further "adopt or maintain such measures as required ... to check the traffic in persons ... for the purposes of prostitution."

With regard to persons who have been trafficked, the convention emphasizes their protection and safe repatriation I calls on state parties "so far as possible" to "make suitabl provisions for trafficking victims" temporary care an maintenance"; to repatriate such persons "only afte agreement ... with the State of destination"; and, wher persons cannot pay the costs of repatriation, to bear the cos "as far as the neares frontier". While we recognize the righ of governments to make and enforce laws regulating nationa borders, they must distinguish between those wh purposefully violate immigration laws and others who ar victims for forced trafficking.

The obligation of state parties to take all appropria measure to suppress the traffic in women was later reiterate in the 1979 Convention on the Elimination of All Forms Discrimination Against Women (CEDAW). CEDAW do not, however, elaborate upon specific steps. Like t Trafficking Convention, CEDAW links trafficking to t exploitation of prostitution, but fails to address trafficki for other exploitative ends, such as coerced marriage a forced labour.

Although trafficking in women and girls had become lucrative and expanding cross border trade, it routine escapes effective national and international sanctio Trafficking for the purposes of forced prostitution h frequently been mischaracterized by governments a human rights organizations alike as a voluntary a presuming the women's consent, even when ample evider is available to the contrary. Both forced prostitution a coerced marriage also have largely been dismissed as crin perpetrated by private individuals for which Sta undertake no responsibility under international human rights law.

We in India have drafted a bill to be put up at the SAARC summit meeting to be held in Colombo, Sri Lanka in July, 1998. Some of the salient features of the draft convention are:

In the recently held Ninth SAARC Summit at Male in May 12–14, 1997, the Prime Minister of Bangladesh Sheikh Hasina categorically asserted that steps should be taken by all SAARC countries against trafficking in women and children. The Declaration of the Ninth SAARC Summit in its section on women in development stated, "Expressing grave concern at the trafficking of come and children within and between countries, the Heads of State of Governments pledged to coordinate their efforts and take effective measures to address this problem. They decided that existing legislation in Member-States should be strengthened and strictly enforced. This should include simplification of repatriation procedures for victims of trafficking. They also decided that the feasibility of establishing a Regional Convention on Combatting the Crime of Trafficking in Women and Children for Prostitution should be examined by the relevant Technical Committee".

CONCLUSIONS

This paper set out to provide some empirical data on the attitudes, motivations and activities of male British sex tourists, rather than to develop a theoretical analysis either of these men or of the phenomenon of sex tourism. However, I will end with some brief comments on theoretical issues.

In particular, I wish to take issue with those analyses which give primacy to the concept of patriarchy in discussions of sex tourism and prostitution, for it seems to me that this concept alone is not enough to explain the attitudes, motivations and activities of British male sex tourists.

Radical feminists hold that 'sexuality is gendered as gender sexualised... the exoticisation of dominance and submission creates gender... Thus, the sex difference and the dominance-submission dynamic define each other.' (MacKinnon, 1988:107, see also Jeffreys, 1990).

Although, I believe that British sex tourists provide a very clear example of how a masculine identity can be expressed, reinforced and constructed through a given sexual practice, I think it would be wrong to conclude that the power these men exercise is simply or even primarily patriarchal. Their power is also 'racialised' and its currency is economic, and it is only if we recognise this that we can develop analyses of sex tourism that can accommodate the unpalatable fact that not all sex tourists are heterosexual and not all sex tourists are men.

It is also clear that male sex tourists are not the only group of people to derive benefits from sex tourism. Its economic benefits for national and international capital are equally, if not more, striking. As well as being part of the planned economic development of a number of South East Asian countries, providing a vital source of foreign exchange and substantial profits for local entrepreneurs, national and international travel, tourist and leisure companies, I would argue that sex tourism plays a broader economic role, contributing to an on-going process of primitive accumulation.

A number of Marxist theorists have argued that non-capitalist modes of production have been artificially preserved in under-developed countries, and that these household economies supply cheap labour to the capitalist system. Potts (1990: 188) summarises as follows:

According to the requirements of capitalism, [the worker] is either incorporated—in various ways—into the capitalist productive process or thrown back into the household. This household feeds the worker during unproductive periods and thus reproduces the worker's labour power.

In this way, reproduction takes place at no cost to capital. In Thailand, it seems that a prostitution economy serves precisely this same function, for not only are women thrown into this economy whenever their labour is surplus to capital's requirements, but also women's sexual labour often wholly or partly supports the households that furnish both national and international capital with a cheap, disposable workforce.

To argue that sex tourism, or indeed any other form of prostitution, exists in order to ensure that men can buy 'the sex act' and so exercise patriarchal rights of access to women's bodies (see Pateman, 1988:199) deflects attention from these economic and social relations, yet it is precisely upon these relations that the power men like Bert (quoted at the start of this paper) exercise over Thai prostitutes rests upon. Analyses which view patriarchy as *the locus* of social power also create political problems when applied to sex tourism. If prostitution is seen as a form of sexual oppression rather than of economic exploitation, it follows that 'Free prostitution does not exist, whatever the means of exercising it... prostitution of women [is] always by force... it is a violation of human rights and an outrage to the dignity of women (Barry, 1991, quoted in Van der Gaag, 1994).

As well as drawing radical feminists into direct conflict with most grassroots prostitute organisations campaigning to develop, extend and protect the rights of sex workers (a project which necessarily involves a view of prostitution as a form of paid work and also, therefore, a recognition of women's individual freedom to choose this route to economic survival), such a position obscures all distinctions between prostitutes and the very different social relations which govern their work (see Truong, 1990).

In reality, the term 'prostitution embraces an enormous range of activities undertaken on very different terms and under very different conditions, and for reasons of political strategy it is vital to distinguish between them.

My own view is that while sex tourism must be recognised as first and foremost a form of economic exploitation, it should also be seen as a unique and distinctive form of exploitation. There are fundamental differences between capitalist employers and purchasers of sex which must be borne in mind in any programme of political resistance.

The relationship between capital and labour is characterised by a mutual dependence as well as antagonism. Without a class of wage workers, capital accumulation cannot take place. But though sex tourists exercise economic power over prostitutes, there is no mutual economic dependency between the two groups. Thai prostitutes need sex tourists in order to subsist but sex tourists would not actually starve, wither or die without Thai prostitutes.

Since sex tourists as a collective group are not locked into a dialectical relationship with these women, it would be extremely difficult for prostitutes to win concessions through struggle with these men, who can simply move their custom elsewhere.

It is not sex tourists but governments, international travel companies, hoteliers, local business people and so on who have an economic interest in maintaining the flow of sex tourists, so to engage in direct action against sex tourists (as some feminist and guerrilla organisations do—see Lee, 1991), satisfying as it may be, will not necessarily improve the lot of the women who sell their sexual labour.

The phenomenon of sex tourism reveals all too graphically the nature of the relationship between underdeveloped countries at the periphery of 'regional political economies' (Cohen, 1987) and those at their centre.

It also rests upon the articulation of structures, ideologies and sexualities that are simultaneously gendered and 'racialised'. Sex tourism represents an immense theoretical challenge for both feminists and Marxists, as well as an urgent political one.

Prevention requires international coordination in law enforcement, policy, programmes and campaigning and we, as campaigners, should be keeping up with trends in campaigning techniques and methods, including evaluating our impact on a national, regional and global scale.

In developing their 2001-2003 national campaign against the sexual exploitation of children in tourism, the Brazilian Tourist Board (EMBRATUR) in collaboration with various Governmental and non-Governmental organizations strategically decided that the campaign should be informative and direct, but the tone would not be aggressive or negative. The material would be kept simple, not cluttered with text, and images of children would not be used.

Its goal is to win visitors about the severity of Brazilian laws against child sex tourism, and to invite conscientious citizens to help in the fight against this abuse by providing a toll free reporting hotline. An initial evaluation, strategically conducted during Carnival, are positive and reveal optimistic numbers regarding its impact.

In terms of reducing the extent of child sexual exploitation by tourists in Cuba, there are some fairly straightforward short term steps that could be taken. The major sending countries are Canada, Italy and Spain. It seems that many of the men who sexually exploit children are frequent visitors to Cuba and it also appears that many of them fund their trips through smuggling. Simply by taking more active steps to police this illegal activity, customs officials in sending countries could help to reduce the ease with which such men satisfy their tastes.

It is also the case that many sex tourists are ignorant of the age of consent laws in Cuba and mistakenly believe that 'anything goes' in this 'sexual permissive' country. Publicising the actual law may help to deter some of them. However, so long as there is no extra-territorial law which allows for their prosecution back home and so long as the Cuban authorities continue to persecute and punish child prostitutes rather than their clients, it seems likely that men like Charlie and Mark will continue to feel secure about sexually exploiting children.

In the longer term, it may also be that we can learn something about sex tourists' propensity to sexually exploit children by turning the question on its head and asking questions about those men who do not use under-age prostitutes. In Cuba, we interviewed two men whom we believe had not sexually exploited and would not sexually exploit children. Both were Canadians in professional occupations and both were divorcees in their forties. One of these men had spent a month doing voluntary work in an agricultural collective and was spending two weeks in Varedero to relax before returning home, the other was an administrator in a psychiatric hospital on a three week vacation. The first had a relationship with a Cuban woman, also in her forties, whilst working on the collective. In Varedero, he befriended two 13 years old prostitutes from Havana, buying them food and chatting with them in the bars where they solicited but did not have sex with them. The second struck up a friendship with Lola, with whom he danced, bought meals for and invited to use the shower in his hotel room but did not have sexual intercourse with her.

Both of these men were more knowledgeable and informed about the political and economic situation in Cuba than the average tourist and both appeared to be genuinely disturbed by the prevalence of child prostitution. They did not talk about Cuban women and girls as 'racialised' or sexual 'others', rather they would compare the situation of children in Varedero to that of children in Canada and they understood the difference to be a consequence of structural factors (economic, political and social) not nature.

'Opportunity' did not make a 'thief' of these men. Why? Clearly they did not regard the sexual availability of 13 and 14 years old girls as an 'opportunity', and this in turn implies that they do not buy into an ideology which insists that a 'real man' must have sexual intercourse with any female on offer, or into an ideology which dehumanises 'racialised' others.

So long as poverty is imposed on large numbers of people in economically underdeveloped countries. Western tourists will be provided with 'opportunities' to sexually exploit and abuse children.

As well as having a responsibility to take more active steps to police those who take advantage of this situation, it seems to us that western governments have a moral responsibility to make some attempt to eradicate the kind of ideologies which teach their male citizens to view the misery and desperation of children like Anna-Bel as representing nothing more than an 'opportunity' to indulge their own sexual fantasies.

□□□